Strategies for Effective Enrollment Management

FRANK R. KEMERER   J. VICTOR BALDRIDGE   KENNETH C. GREEN

American Association of State Colleges and Universities

© American Association of State Colleges and Universities
One Dupont Circle/Suite 700
Washington, DC 20036

Library of Congress Cataloging in Publications Data

Kemerer, Frank R.
  Strategies for effective enrollment management.

  Bibliography: p.
    1. Universities and colleges—United States—Admission.
I. Baldridge, J. Victor. II. Green, Kenneth C. III. Title.
LB2351.2.K45   1982   378'.1059'73   82-18474
ISBN 0-88044-062-7

Table of Contents

Figures

Tables

Preface

The academic community confronts two major problems in the 1980s: declining enrollments and a changing perspective on federal and state support for higher education. Either alone would be enough to produce a sense of insecurity. Together, they threaten to bring a new depression to American higher education.

For several years we have conducted comprehensive research on higher education enrollments. In part, our work has had a practical focus. Not only did we want to know more about the dimension of the enrollment problem, but we also wanted to uncover management strategies that would enable institutions to manage their enrollments successfully.

This book directly concerns the practical side of our research. We must admit to a particular bias at the start. We believe individual campuses have—and should have—the capacity to respond to their own student recruitment and retention problems. State agencies and state coordinating bodies have final authority in some states over enrollments at many institutions, but considerable initiative remains at the local campus to reverse downward trends before a pattern sets in that will prompt central agencies to act. Throughout the book, then, our discussion is based on an institutional perspective.

Although this book was commissioned by the American Association of State Colleges and Universities (AASCU), it addresses the enrollment problems of all types of institutions. The contents are by no means directed solely to admissions office personnel. In fact, part of the reason campuses have enrollment problems is that student recruitment and retention are too often viewed as a concern only of the office of admissions. Consequently, we are directing this book to college and university presidents and vice presidents, as well as directors of admissions.

Deans and department chairpersons concerned about their own enrollment problems will also find much of value in this book.

Readers looking for short-cuts through easy-to-follow formulas, quick-fix solutions, or miracle cures will be disappointed. In our view, there is no such panacea. Successful enrollment management requires hard work by administrators and faculty. What we offer in this book are some insights and strategies that will both make the job easier and increase the likelihood of success.

A Word about the Research

In the spring and summer of 1981 we conducted a national survey of 760 college presidents and 760 admissions directors. Seventy-three percent of the presidents and 70 percent of the admissions directors returned the questionnaires. For AASCU institutions, the figures were 84 percent and 80 percent, respectively. The survey is referred to throughout the book as the "1981 National Enrollment Survey." We focused on three major types of public and private institutions: universities, four-year colleges, and two-year colleges. Survey data have been weighted to reflect approximately 2,500 institutions. The Spencer Foundation of Chicago underwrote most of the survey research costs, with supplemental funding provided by North Texas State University.

Under a grant provided by the American Association of State Colleges and Universities, we also conducted case studies around the country at a number of institutions that have had success with some aspect of enrollment management. Included are case studies of the State University of New York (SUNY) colleges at Potsdam and Geneseo, California State University at Long Beach, Old Dominion University, Alfred University, Bradley University, Pace University, and Mercy College.

Funding from the W. K. Kellogg Foundation of Battle Creek, Michigan, facilitated our study of student retention. Utilizing these funds, the Higher Education Research Institute (HERI) at the University of California at Los Angeles (UCLA) has formed a consortium of eight southern California liberal arts colleges, which are seeking ways to reduce costly student attrition. The members of the consortium include Azusa Pacific College, Chapman College, Harvey Mudd College, Loyola Marymount University, Mount St. Mary's College, Pitzer College, Scripps College, and Whittier College.

Acknowledgments

We are particularly grateful to the four organizations providing funds for this work—the Spencer Foundation of Chicago, the American Association of State Colleges and Universities, the W. K. Kellogg Foundation of Battle Creek, and North Texas State University. We are also grateful to the Higher Education Research Institute at UCLA, from which the enrollment management study was coordinated.

In addition to these organizations, several persons deserve special thanks for their assistance. H. Thomas James of the Spencer Foundation was in many respects the father of the project. Because of his strong interest in maintaining institutional quality and adaptability, he encouraged with words and money our efforts to investigate the enrollment crisis. Harold Delaney of AASCU and Robert Toulouse of North Texas State University strongly desired to support research that could be helpful for state institutions. Peter Ellis of the Kellogg Foundation indirectly helped this project by funding the eight-college retention consortium in southern California, from which we learned much about institutional response to enrollment difficulties. Charles Marshall, Executive Director of the National Association of College Admissions Counselors, and J. Douglas Conner, Executive Director of the American Association of Collegiate Registrars and Admissions Officers, provided valuable commentary with regard to several chapters in Part One. So, too, did David W. Chapman, assistant professor at SUNY-Buffalo, who has conducted considerable research on enrollment management, and Bruce Walker, Associate Director of the College Board's Southwestern Regional Office. We appreciate the encouragement, ideas, and trust these people have given us.

We are also indebted to those persons at our case study institutions who helped make our visits so insightful. Our research assistants Sheri Smith and Pat Okimi, doctoral candidates at North Texas State University, and Linda Mintz, a research assistant at HERI and a doctoral candidate at UCLA, are to be thanked for their hard work. Pat Okimi deserves special thanks for her excellent case study reports and her insights on strategic planning. We also want to acknowledge the hard work of our secretaries, Avonna Davis at North Texas State University and Robin Braum and Terry Weiner at HERI. Finally, Betsy Kielman of AASCU is to be congratulated for her efficiency and commitment in directing the publication stages of this book.

Frank R. Kemerer
Denton, Texas

J. Victor Baldridge
Malibu, California

Kenneth C. Green
Los Angeles, California

September 1, 1982

CHAPTER 1
Basic Issues and Themes

The past thirty years have been marked by a continuing state of self-proclaimed crisis and financial difficulty in American higher education. These "crisis issues" are well-known: the crisis of growth (too much, too little, and finally none); the problem of doctorates (too few and then too many); the problem of faculty unions; the crisis of accountability; and the consequences of inflation. Yet American higher education has been surprisingly resilient, surviving and actually thriving during periods of challenge.

The 1980s present a new set of challenges for higher education. The academic community confronts two major problems: striking shifts that will produce declining enrollments and economic difficulties that will mark changes in the financial future of American colleges and universities.

In this first chapter, we review enrollment trends and projections, examining their implications for different types of colleges and universities. Included is a discussion of some of our survey data, which suggest that campus presidents may be overly optimistic about the future and may not be moving quickly enough to counter shifting enrollment patterns. The chapter concludes by addressing the basic themes of the book.

The Difficulty of Predicting Enrollment Trends

At first, it seems easy to predict future enrollment patterns. The novice assumes that the proper way to estimate enrollments is simply to chart the size of the college-age cohort. The Census Bureau can give this simple information. If that were the scope of the problem, anyone could make an accurate prediction about

1

future college enrollments. In reality, the problem is considerably more complex. Literally dozens of variables influence the size of the college population.

An Exercise: Predicting Enrollment Patterns

We have developed an exercise for our enrollment management workshops to show the complexity of the prediction problem. You might find it interesting to stop, take out a pencil, and complete the exercise. (If you do not, at least look at the results from one recent workshop, which are presented in the next section.)

Here are the instructions for the exercise (see Table 1):

1. List all the factors you think you would need to answer this question: "What will my state's total higher education enrollment be in five years?" (Examples of factors: size of high school graduating class, percentage of high school graduates going on to college, unemployment rate, size of 18-22 year old age cohort.)

2. In the appropriate columns, rate on a scale from 1 (low) to 10 (high) the following:

    •   **Current accuracy** of information you have on each factor.

    •   **Five-year prediction:** your current ability to predict with accuracy what this factor will be in five years.

    •   **Manipulability:** your college's ability to influence and shape each factor.

Results of a Typical Workshop Group

Table 2 is a completed version of the chart. It includes factors listed at a recent workshop, including the participants' ratings on the reliability of current information, their ability to predict these factors five years hence, and their college's ability to manipulate the factors. Several trends are obvious from this chart.

1. In order to predict enrollment patterns accurately, one needs information about many variables. Actually, the workshop

Table 1: An Exercise in Predicting College Enrollment

| | Rating Scale 1-10 (1 = Low) | | |
Factors Necessary For Accurate Prediction	Current Info.	5-Year Predictions	Able to Manipulate

Table 2: One Seminar's List and Average Ratings
on Enrollment Predictions

Rating Scale 1-10

Factors Necessary For Accurate Prediction	Current Info.	5-Year Predictions	Able to Manipulate
Present High School Graduates Going on to College	9	4	3
Birthrates	10	9	0
Unemployment (Demand for Labor: School Options)	7	3	0
Draft Policy	10	2	0
High School Graduation Rates	10	7	1
Cost of Living (Inflation Impacts, Ability to Pay)	6	2	0
Financial Aid Policies	9	4	2
Cohort Size (# of 18-22 Year Olds)	10	8	0
Composition of College-Age Cohort (Racial/ Ethnic Mix)	9	8	0
Percentage of "New Clientele" (Adults, Minorities) Going to College	5	2	4
Retention/Attrition Rates	8	3	5
State Financial Aid Policies	8	6	3
Mix of Vocational/ Academic Demand	9	3	2

participants named nearly three times the number of factors on this list, but we condensed them. What this list suggests is that merely knowing the size of the age cohort will not allow one to predict college enrollments.

2. The reliability of current information is fairly high. Most people rated current information somewhere between 6 and 10, with most scores in the upper range.

3. The reliability of current data for making five-year projections, however, dropped off very sharply. Look at the difference between the first and second columns. In general, the participants had much lower faith in their ability to project five years in the future.

4. Now look at the last column. The workshop participants were quite pessimistic about their ability to manipulate the factors. Only one factor got as high as 5—retention and attrition rates. This is one reason we highlight retention strategies in a later chapter. Other factors listed range from low manipulability to absolutely none!

Predicting enrollment patterns is actually bewilderingly complex. If it were simple, commentators would not have been wrong for the past decade! Prophets of doom have been declaring since at least 1970 that higher education enrollment would drop sharply. That crisis refused to materialize in the 1970s. Now, however, the realities are becoming more pressing. We may actually be standing on the threshold of a substantial downturn in enrollments. In the next section we examine trends that indicate that the decline may be about to begin for many institutions.

Enrollment Trends and Institutional Futures*

It seems clear that the future of American higher education through the end of the century will be profoundly affected by

---

*A more detailed discussion of material in this section can be found Baldridge, Kemerer, and Green, 1982.

the predicted 23 percent aggregate decline in the size of the traditional college-age cohort between 1980 and 1996.

What is not so clear, however, is exactly what the consequences will be for specific institutions. Moreover, the nation's recent economic problems, which have prompted significant shifts in state and federal social program expenditures, further compound the uncertainty over institutional futures.

Variations in College Enrollment Projections

Carol Shulman has observed that enrollment projections "vary greatly because the analysts build into their forecasts differing *visions* of how higher education can and should develop and because their visions are linked to special assumptions about the future of the American economy and its relationship to higher education" (Schulman, 1976, p. 13). Projection methods range from the simple to the complex. The National Center for Education Statistics has used *constant growth rate* measures to forecast enrollments, generally ignoring external variables such as financial aid policies and economic factors (National Center for Education Statistics, 1976). The Carnegie Foundation (1975) and the Carnegie Council (1980) have included enrollment trends as well as external factors in their projections. Several analysts focus on the *economic incentives* for college attendance and suggest that, in addition to demographic factors, a declining job market and a lower "economic rate of return" on a college education will produce enrollment decline (O'Toole, 1977; Dresch, 1975). Others, such as Howard Bowen (1974) and Leslie and Miller (1974), suggest that postsecondary institutions could play a much broader role in American society, thus contributing to increased enrollments.

These factors and others are reflected in the enrollment projections offered by a number of analysts, as shown in Figure 1. The forecasts range from overly optimistic to extremely pessimistic. Some suggest little change whereas others imply that extreme measures are necessary.

Undergraduate Enrollments. Undergraduate enrollments are the element of higher education most directly affected by demographic trends. In fall 1980, 91 percent of all first-time, full-time college freshmen were either 18 or 19 years old. The 18-24 age cohort constitutes 80 percent of all undergraduate enrollment.

Figure 1. Projections for Total Enrollment in
Postsecondary Education to 1990
*(in millions, relative to actual 1977 total
enrollment of 11.4 million)*

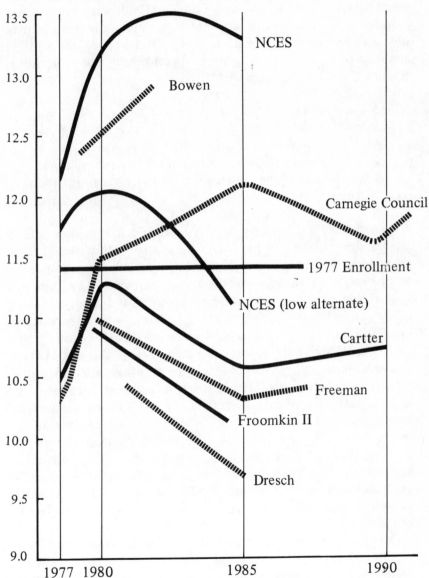

Note: The lines for Bowen, Freeman, Dresch, and Froomkin's second scenario are not based on actual figures but instead are an approximate illustration of their views. *Source:* Centra, 1980, Fig. 2.

Graduate Enrollments. Few observers have said much recently about graduate enrollment prospects, perhaps reflecting a silent consensus that the recent problems in the academic labor market will worsen, thereby contributing to further enrollment decline. Yet the Carnegie Council (1980) anticipates stable enrollment or only slight declines in graduate enrollments over the next twenty years. This optimism is based on the shift in graduate education from academic apprenticeships to professional training. The council states that

> *too much has been made of too little. . . . We have heard mostly about the less than 10 percent of graduate work that is in deep trouble (the academic Ph.D.) and less about the other more than 90 percent that has been moving along unimpaired or has even prospered (Carnegie Council, 1980, p. 48).*

Although the decline of the academic job market affects graduate enrollments, it has been field specific rather than generalized. Some disciplines have found favor in industry and government (e.g., economics), and others, such as computer science and engineering, continue to experience high demand. Too, humanists have found outlets for their skills and talents in the private sector (see Solmon, Kent, Ochsner, and Hurwicz, 1981). Graduate education will probably be very volatile during the next twenty years, especially within degree levels and across disciplines.

Regional Impacts. The aggregate demographic data also hide important regional differences. The 1980 census shows the continued growth of the Sunbelt states at the expense of the urban Northeast and Midwest. The Western Interstate Commission on Higher Education (1979) notes there will be significant regional differences in the decline in the number of high school graduates between 1979 and 1995. The Northeast and Northcentral regions will suffer the greatest decline, whereas the southern and western states will experience the least. Yet even the regional data mask some important state differences: the pattern of projected high school graduates in the western states is strongly affected by a 30 percent decline in the number of high school graduates in California.

The Carnegie Council has been specific about the individual states, categorizing them according to their enrollment problems. Six Frostbelt states are forecast to have much *worse* than average enrollment problems over the next fifteen years; Alaska plus six Sunbelt states are expected to fare much *better* than the national average (see Figure 2).

Looking at the Trends from the Institutional Perspective

Analysts agree that the "enrollment crisis" of the 1980s will have differential impacts on institutions. Some campuses will experience no decline and may even report some increase in enrollment; others will be severely hurt by the demographic events of the 1980s.

The two types of institutions considered to be most adversely affected by enrollment problems in the 1980s are small, private liberal arts colleges and private two-year colleges. The least vulnerable institutions seem to be research universities, selective liberal arts colleges, and public two-year institutions. Comprehensive and doctoral degree-granting institutions should have enrollment patterns somewhat between the extremes of universities and private two-year colleges. The vast majority of the vulnerable institutions are private colleges. According to the Carnegie Council, "only about 10 of the over 700 institutions in the most vulnerable categories are public" (1980, p. 61).

Private institutions are more vulnerable to enrollment problems than their public sector counterparts for a number of reasons. These institutions, particularly the less selective liberal arts and two-year colleges, are concentrated in the Frostbelt states, which will experience severe drops in the 18-24 age cohort over the next fifteen years. These institutions have also been hard hit by the high inflation of recent years. In many instances short-term savings gained by deferred plant maintenance, retrenchment, and low faculty salaries will have long-term consequences. Changing federal and state financial aid policies, particularly in the Guaranteed Student Loan (GSL) programs, will further erode the ability of these institutions to recruit middle-income students.

Mid-level public institutions, many of them former teacher colleges, may also experience enrollment problems. They had some difficulties during the brief enrollment downturn of the early 1970s, "and that experience sets the stage for even more

10

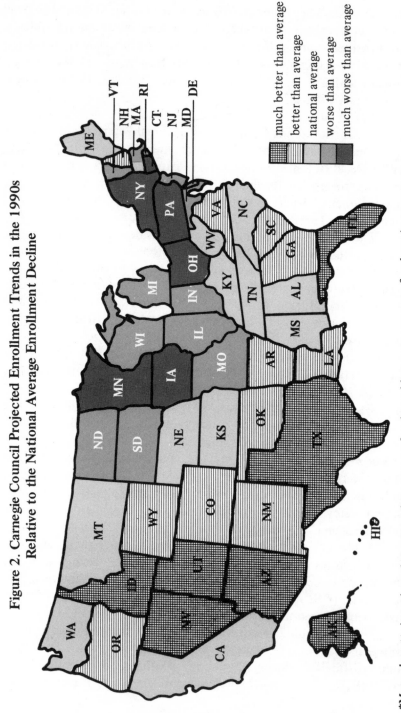

Figure 2. Carnegie Council Projected Enrollment Trends in the 1990s
Relative to the National Average Enrollment Decline

*Massachusetts is projected as worse than average for the public sector: average for the private sector.
Source: Carnegie Council on Policy Studies in Higher Education, 1980.

drastic change in the next fifteen years" (Glenny, 1980, p. 375). They will probably have to compete with two-year institutions, although they are somewhat less prepared than community colleges to serve students interested in short-term, technical/vocational training.

Financial Issues

What distinguishes the financial problems of the 1980s from those in prior periods of financial exigency is that the current ones will occur concurrently with an enrollment downturn. During previous periods of financial difficulty, such as the "New Depression" years (Cheit, 1971), institutions could generally rely on increases in enrollment-driven revenues regardless of shifts in government programs and funding priorities. During the 1980s, however, higher education may experience a real financial depression brought about by the devastating combination of enrollment declines and real reductions in state and federal support.

Federal Support. The "Reagan Revolution" promises to have a major impact on the financial future of both private and public institutions. Virtually no area of the federal higher education budget—from student aid to library development grants to scientific research—has escaped the budget-cutting proposals that have swept through Washington since January 1981.

State Support. Furman (1981) presents a concise summary of recent events affecting state support for higher education. These include not only inflated- but also real-dollar declines in tax revenues, tax revenue shortfalls leading to mid-year budget recessions, a declining share of state appropriations, and shifting social program priorities. Taken together, these events, plus the demographic shifts of the coming decade, do not bode well for strong state financial support for public or private higher education. The Reagan Administration plan to shift many federal social programs to the states will further stimulate the already intense competition for shrinking state funds for postsecondary education.

College Presidents' Concerns about Enrollments

Fears abound that colleges face enrollment shortfalls, budgetary crises, and faculty layoffs. Do college presidents and admissions officers believe these dire predictions will really come true? Our survey of both groups shows an underlying concern, beneath the overt optimism (Table 3).

Sixty percent agree "enrollment is a major concern," and 75 percent report their institutions have suffered from increased competition for students since 1976 (72 percent in public institutions, 83 percent in private). But simultaneously, presidents predict a fairly rosy enrollment picture. Presidents may be concerned but nevertheless expect their institutions to weather the storm. Forty-two percent expect *increases* in their enrollments by 1986, and only 17 percent expect declines!

Presidents felt the financial impact of declining budget cuts in student aid will have more impact than enrollment difficulties. Presidents tend to be guardedly optimistic about enrollments but considerably more worried about overall finances. Twenty-six percent of the presidents felt their institutions faced "fair or poor" financial prospects over the next five years. And admissions directors, who were also surveyed, strongly agreed with the dim financial forecast: 40 percent think major financial aid cuts will have a severe impact on their institutions.

Different Futures for Different Types of Colleges

On one hand, some presidents see enrollment declines: those of private two-year colleges (33 percent) and private universities (27 percent). On the other hand, some presidents face the future with optimism about enrollment *increases:* 57 percent of community college presidents forecast enrollment increases, and 38 percent of presidents at AASCU institutions and private four-year colleges see increases.

One finding is the surprising optimism of presidents of some colleges, which, according to most estimates, will face the worst declines. The four-year private colleges are the prime case. Thirty-nine percent of their presidents foresee enrollment increases and "very good or excellent" finances; most of the rest see the situation "unchanged." Why this optimism in the face of many dire predictions?

Many college presidents seem to assume that their institutions will be immune to the 25 percent decline in the traditional college age group over the next fifteen years. Presidents seem more sensitive to financial issues than to enrollment concerns. Finances are clearly a major issue, considering the massive federal

Table 3: Presidential Perspectives on Enrollments and Finances, by Institutional Type
(percentages)

Survey Question	Public Research Univ.	AASCU Inst.	Public 2-Year Coll.	Private Univ.	Private 4-Year Coll.	Private 2-Year Coll.	All Inst.
1. Concerned About Enrollments	60	55	48	69	68	78	60
2. Enrollment Forecast, 1981-1986*							
Increase over 15 percent	6	0	9	0	6	0	6
Increase 6-14 percent	18	32	48	9	32	22	36
Steady ±5 percent	64	45	34	77	42	44	41
Decrease 6-14 percent	18	17	8	15	17	33	15
Decrease over 15 percent	1	0	1	0	2	0	1
3. Financial Health of Institution in 1980s*							
Excellent	0	5	5	15	8	0	6
Very good	27	20	25	31	30	22	26
Good	36	38	49	46	37	44	42
Fair	36	33	28	7	28	33	22
Poor	0	3	3	0	6	0	4

*Totals may not equal 100 due to rounding error.

cuts that may undermine many colleges' financial solvency. Fifty-two percent of the presidents of liberal arts colleges anticipate *increased* enrollments over the next five years, a startling fact since these are the institutions that will be severely affected by the demographic events of the 1980s. As one admissions director commented in our interviews:

> *Many presidents seem to have the 'last survivor mentality'; they think their institution will be the one that escapes the enrollment problems. In fact, many private liberal arts colleges will have serious difficulties in the coming years.*

Most of our survey respondents felt that, although many public institutions will experience enrollment and financial difficulties in the 1980s, as a group they should fare better than their counterparts in the private sector. Public institutions may experience financial difficulties because of reduced state subsidies not necessarily because of significant declines in their enrollment.

Admissions Directors' Worries about Financial Aid Cuts

Budget cuts will mean that low-income students get less aid and many middle-income students may get none. Cuts in aid programs may reduce enrollments in many institutions as students seek to reduce their college costs by enrolling part-time, living at home, or selecting less expensive colleges. Enrollment problems in the private sector will be further aggravated by the pending cuts in many aid programs, since many of those programs traditionally help students attending independent institutions.

The survey of admissions directors reveals that cuts in financial aid programs will have differential impacts. Admissions directors anticipate that cuts in the Pell Grant program will have a severe impact on 28 percent of public institutions and 51 percent of private institutions, changes in the GSL program will have an adverse effect on enrollments in 22 percent of public colleges and 70 percent of private colleges, and reductions in state aid programs will have a severe impact on enrollments in 20 percent of public institutions and 62 percent of private colleges. These views have probably become even more pessimistic now in light of continued cutbacks in student aid programs.

To summarize, the surveys show that college presidents are remarkably optimistic in spite of the widely predicted enrollment crisis. The vast majority believe their enrollment will either remain the same or increase; only 16 percent anticipate drops. The admissions directors, however, are not so optimistic. By and large, presidents seem more concerned about finances than enrollments. That pessimistic outlook is largely shared by admissions directors.

False Optimism and Lack of Preparation?

One president we interviewed said that presidents in public speeches, in their responses to questionnaires, and in their addresses before legislatures put on a "good face" for the public. In public they predict solid enrollments for the future, but in private their assessments are considerably less optimistic.

Is this optimism of presidents, however feigned, preventing them from making adequate preparation? In later chapters we will comment on survey results about preparation but let us mention several patterns here. First, there is considerable action around offices of admissions. Recruiting activities are being increased, new staff are being added, and more attention is being directed to the position of the office of admissions in the organization chart. On the other hand, little attention seems to be directed to student retention. Chapters two through five explore these topics in considerable depth.

Second, colleges are hiring more part-time faculty, and presidents report in interviews that the reason is "flexibility" in case faculty have to be laid-off. To some people this seems like a shortsighted policy that reduces institutional quality, but to others hiring part-timers seems a necessary evil to prepare for an uncertain future. The part-time faculty issue is discussed in chapter seven. Other quality issues are addressed in chapter eight.

Third, in other personnel areas there is surprisingly little effort to prepare for possible enrollment problems. There appears to be little emphasis on early retirement programs for faculty, a lack of preparation for retrenchment and lay-off activities, and little attention to a wide range of other important personnel matters. Chapter seven will discuss this lack of preparation.

In some ways, then, it seems that campuses are taking steps to bolster their enrollment situations. But on the whole, both our surveys and some of our on-site case studies convinced us that there is little comprehensive effort to prepare for anticipated enrollment declines.

Institutional Adaptability

We do not believe that environmental forces rigidly determine an institution's destiny. We believe that an active, aggressive stance will allow institutions to adjust to the coming future. However, a realistic assessment suggests that well-planned action is needed, and is needed now if future events are not to overwhelm many campuses. Certainly there are many institutions that are already making aggressive preparations for the future. A few have even faced the spectre of their own demise and managed to bounce back. The case studies we have selected for presentation throughout this book often discuss situations where institutions faced extreme difficulties and managed to rebound. Let us look briefly at one.

Bradley University, a private university of 5,500 students in Illinois with both liberal arts and technical programs, suffered an unexpected enrollment shortfall in the early 1970s necessitating the retrenchment of one-third the faculty. To avoid being caught unaware again, the university, under the leadership of President Martin Abegg, took vigorous action. Major initiatives included the following:

- The hiring of a new director of admissions experienced in both admissions and marketing to guide the revitalization of the office of admissions.

- The development of a new concept called student life planning designed to serve student needs from the point of initial contact in the field through the admissions and orientation process, declaration of a major, and graduation.

- The reorganization of campus administration, eliminating the student affairs vice president and creating a new unit called Student Life Planning, which grouped offices related to student recruitment, retention, and placement together under the direction of the vice president of academic affairs.

- The diverting of resources to support new initiatives in the student life planning unit as well as a major upgrading of university publications.

These changes resulted in a remarkable enrollment turnaround. From 1975 to 1981, the number of applications for admission increased by 49 percent, new student enrollment increased by 21 percent, American College Testing (ACT) scores moved from a composite of 21 to 23, freshmen retention reached 85 percent, and the percentage of students graduating on time moved from below the national average (50 percent) to 65 percent. Bradley University confronts the perilous 1980s positively and with a belief that it can continue to assert substantial control over its destiny.

Basic Themes of the Book

Let's stand back from the Bradley University case study for a moment and see what can be learned from it. In the face of serious enrollment threats Bradley managed to rebound, to thrive. Bradley's experience sets the basic theme for this book: that in the face of environmental challenges institutions can adapt and thrive. Part of that adaptation is a psychological attitude about how to approach the future. From our interviews and research we think that successful institutions have had aggressive leadership that adopted certain frames of mind. We believe that in order to adapt successfully, institutions must do the following:

1. *Take an active, assertive stance.* Although environment and demographic patterns are the primary factors in the

changing situation, institutions nevertheless can help shape their own futures by the actions they take. They are not merely pawns in the hands of fate.

2. *Make a realistic assessment of barriers, but refuse to let the barriers halt progress.* Clearly we are not advocating a naive optimism that fails to acknowledge and assess real barriers. The ostrich mentality of many overly optimistic administrators seems foolish. There are indeed real barriers and real problems, but their realistic appraisal does not mean succumbing to despair.

3. *Develop a set of concrete, practical steps specifically designed to enhance enrollment management.* We think that most institutions can significantly upgrade their enrollment management activities, and Part One of the book focuses on some very practical steps that can be taken to accomplish that improvement.

4. *Adopt a "strategic planning" approach.* One of the most obvious things about our case studies was that most of the successful institutions had shifted away from the sterility of conventional long-range planning. Instead, they were much more oriented to "strategic" planning—assessing the environment, adapting quickly, and matching institutional activities with market demands. This shift in basic administrative approach is discussed in the latter half of the book.

5. *Maintain a focus on fundamental institutional vitality and quality, not on "quick-fix" solutions.* One of the things we discovered early was that many institutions had grasped for quick-fix solutions—bringing in marketing consultants, producing flashy publications, and developing gimmicky approaches to build up their enrollments. But most of these quick fixes rapidly came undone. Institutions that were truly successful in adapting to enrollment difficulties made fundamental changes, concentrated on quality issues, and paid careful attention to the professional excellence of their faculty.

These five themes dominate the book. In Part One we look at the concrete activities the campus can undertake to improve student recruitment and retention. In Part Two we look at the more general issues of strategic planning and institutional quality. We have added Part Two because we are convinced that in the long run issues of strategic planning, administrative and faculty excellence, and institutional quality are just as vital as the specific attention to recruitment and retention. In short, we are trying to combine the practical aspects of enrollment management with the overarching issues of institutional vitality and quality.

PART 1
THE DYNAMICS
OF ENROLLMENT
MANAGEMENT

What is enrollment management? Does it mean recruiting and admissions work? Does it refer to a particular marketing strategy? How does an institution manage its enrollment?

In its proper form enrollment management is a broad and sophisticated concept. It is often confused with marketing; however, marketing is just one activity that contributes to successful enrollment management. Enrollment management has both conceptual and procedural components. As a *concept,* enrollment management implies an assertive approach to ensuring the steady supply of qualified students required to maintain institutional vitality. As a *procedure,* enrollment management is a set of activities to help institutions interact more successfully with their potential students.

Enrollment management encompasses at least eight interdependent activities: clarification of institutional mission, program development, marketing, recruiting, admissions, financial aid, orientation, and retention. As the list implies, enrollment management involves a holistic approach, and the components are clearly linked. Good program development depends upon a clear sense of institutional mission. Marketing strategies are developed based on program offerings. Recruitment, admissions, and financial aid efforts are integrated to serve a specific clientele's needs. Orientation programs are an outgrowth of recruitment efforts and facilitate student integration into the academic and student life of the campus. Likewise, retention efforts acknowledge a full range of academic and student life priorities and are linked tightly to recruitment activities.

The Quick-Fix Temptation

Unfortunately, most institutions wait until problems surface before they take action, and then they often attempt to resolve enrollment problems through quick-fix solutions. Kreutner and Godfrey (1980-81) identify this approach as the Scarlett O'Hara syndrome—"I'll worry about it tomorrow." Flashy publications and media blitzes may be mounted; administrators may attend expensive marketing workshops; a marketing firm may be hired; a special campus task force formed to examine enrollment problems. All these responses assume that an enrollment problem is a short-term abberation rather than a sign of a changing relationship between the institution and its potential clientele.

Carried to an extreme, the 'hard sell' marketing approach selected by many colleges and universities can border on the ridiculous. Kotler (1976) cites one public university that seriously considered releasing balloons containing scholarship certificates. Not only are such ill-conceived efforts not likely to produce many new applicants, but they also make the institution appear foolish.

The Need for In-Depth Changes

Enrollment management is the antithesis of the quick-fix and involves much more than increased attention and resources for recruitment activities. In fact, real effectiveness may require some organizational restructuring to integrate enrollment management activities into everyday campus decision-making.

Colleges and universities can exert considerable control over their enrollments in spite of the fact they have little influence over many environmental forces (government policies, unemployment, and shifts in the labor market for college graduates) that affect enrollments. Within the limits of demographic, economic, and political realities, colleges and universities have considerable room to "manage" the flow of students into and through the institution. Glenny and Bowen (1981) identify thirty factors that affect enrollment levels. Of the thirty, two-thirds are subject to at least some institutional control and include such matters as admissions standards, transfer policies, use of part-time faculty, dropout rate, and program costs.

Institutions *can* do something about enrollment patterns; they are *not* entirely passive victims of a fate they cannot control.

But the task is not easy and requires genuine, deep-seated resolve and hard-nosed effort. Part One of this book discusses some practical, concrete steps institutions can take.

It is composed of four chapters, the first of which discusses how enrollment management concerns can be better integrated into campus decision-making. The next three chapters advance practical strategies for revitalizing the office of admissions, improving student recruitment through selective adoption of marketing techniques, and reducing the costly student attrition rate.

CHAPTER 2
Organizing for Enrollment Management

Several organizational problems inevitably arise when enrollment management efforts are begun. The major problems include bottlenecks in the acquisition and sharing of enrollment research data, the lack of communication among campus constituencies, widespread misinformation about the campus enrollment situation, and an absence of effective coordination. Because these problems are rarely addressed effectively, the results of an enrollment management effort are less impressive than they might be. The first task of this chapter is to explore these organizational problems.

The second task of the chapter is to discuss solutions to the problems identified. Four approaches to overcoming organizational difficulties in recruitment and retention are advanced. Although each approach has its own strengths and weaknesses, all promote better integration of enrollment management with campus governance and decision-making.

Problems in Recruitment and Retention Activities

On most campuses, recruitment and retention activities are isolated from the institution's central decision centers. As a result, problems inevitably result when efforts to increase recruitment and retention of students are begun.

Absence of Research Data
Data collection is a critical yet often ignored component of enrollment management efforts. Most administrators do not have ready access to recruitment and retention data. Moreover, the organizational structure impedes the analysis and dissemination

of data that are critical to informed policy-making. In one of our case studies the university spent more than a year waiting for basic retention data because the registrar, admissions office, and student affairs office refused to cooperate with each other. The admissions office would not share academic profile data on entering freshmen with other units. The registrar felt that student records were a "sacred trust" that could not be violated, not even for institutional research. Ultimately, a senior academic administrator interceded and gave the research task to an outside consultant. Problems such as this reflect an organizational chart that stresses the autonomy of individual administrative units. In this university, the lack of coordination badly impeded the information flow to decision-makers.

Lack of Campus Awareness

On many campuses, a sizable portion of the faculty and administration is neither very knowledgeable about campus enrollment problems nor very concerned about them. Yet successful enrollment management requires substantial faculty participation to develop programs, establish articulation agreements with feeder institutions, publicize departmental programs, and provide quality teaching and advising. All these are required to attract students, reduce attrition, and develop loyal alumni.

The faculty is generally not involved in student recruitment and retention, and the office of admissions has little influence over campus governance. Most institutions operate under a traditional organizational scheme in which the admissions office has primary responsibility for maintaining enrollments. However, the operational activities of the admissions office are generally limited to communications with potential students. Admissions personnel do not have much influence over the range of program and policy issues that affect enrollments, such as academic program development, student life programs, and retention efforts.

At the same time, admissions personnel are often keenly aware of institutional problems that adversely affect recruitment efforts. Roger Campbell, Director of Undergraduate Admissions at Northwestern University, observes that most admissions directors "would find the strongest possible arguments for improving . . . academic programs" (Campbell, 1981, p. 11). David Riesman (1975) suggests that the admissions director in the small college has a role that is second only to the president insofar as institutional survival is concerned. Yet admissions directors usually have little influence outside of their own offices. A 1978 study of admissions officers at 350 private colleges and universities showed that one-third favored changes in the academic program at their institution but indicated no changes had been made. The researchers concluded that "a degree of conflict of interest exists between those with responsibility for recruiting students and those responsible for the academic offerings" (Murphy and McGarrity, p. 258).

Additionally, when admissions directors seek additional funds to employ more professional staff or to expand the scope of recruitment efforts, they are often thwarted by other administrators responding to cost-cutting mandates from the president.

Failure to Coordinate Efforts

The increasing specialization of recruitment has tended to separate those responsible for it from other officers directly concerned with student recruitment and admissions. J. Douglas Conner, Executive Director of the American Association of Collegiate Registrars and Admissions Officers (AACRAO), told us in an interview that he is distressed at the lack of information admissions personnel have about financial aid. "It seems to me in this crucial time of budget cuts that intelligent admissions decisions cannot be made without some background and information in terms of available student financial aid, and most admissions officers are simply not in a position to discuss this process articulately." Conner maintains that there must be effective integration and cooperation among the offices of admissions, records, and financial aid yet observes that on large campuses he visited while on a recent study leave, "these units at times were not even communicating with one another."

Coordination must extend as well to retention activities. Although both recruitment and retention efforts affect enrollments, these activities are very different in terms of their position and status on the organizational chart. Recruitment activities are focused in the admissions office. The director of admissions is responsible for the decisions that determine recruitment strategies and activities and is often directly accountable for the success or failure of recruitment efforts.

In contrast, retention is a "dispersed" responsibility. In most institutions retention activities do not have an identifiable administrative center. At least half a dozen constituencies and offices are responsible for some facet of retention activities. Faculty, student life officers, deans, counseling center personnel, academic advisors, study skills counselors, and residence hall coordinators, among others, all have varying degrees of responsibility for retention. Because attrition crosses departmental and organizational boundaries, making efforts to attack attrition and maintain enrollments requires coordinated action involving both academic and student affairs administrators. Yet even on those campuses that have launched concerted efforts to reduce attrition, structural issues often impede implementation efforts.

Enrollment management, which encompasses both recruitment and retention as well as a range of other functions, is not the sole responsibility of one or two offices. Rather, it is the responsibility of the entire campus community.

Without addressing organzational concerns, most institutions will not be able to exercise substantial control over their enrollments. The remainder of this chapter presents four possible models for organizing and coordinating enrollment activities. The models vary considerably in the degree of reorganization they require. At one extreme, the "marketing committee" requires almost no substantial change in current organizational structure. At the other extreme, the "division for enrollment management" requires a complete revamping of the organizational chart.

The Marketing Committee

Roger Campbell (1980) proposes an institutional marketing committee that would have an advisory role in recruitment efforts. Campbell suggests that this committee should stress that the entire campus community be responsible for recruitment. He suggests that the committee membership include the directors of admissions and financial aid, the dean of students, a senior faculty program officer, plus some recognized faculty leaders.

Functions of a Marketing Committee

Campbell urges the institutional marketing committee undertake four tasks: analysis, research, programming, and communication.

The first task is defining the primary and secondary markets for recruitment efforts. This effort draws on student application history, admission-to-enrollment trends, student quality factors, and market responses to campus programs. According to Campbell,

> *Market definition begins near the campus and spreads out. The farther one goes, the likelihood of institutional myth replacing reality increases. The task at hand is to identify some acceptable clues that will allow an institution to sense where its primary market is ending and where the secondary market is beginning (1980, p. 16).*

Primary and secondary markets will be discussed in some depth in chapter four.

Second, the committee's research task focuses on student life and campus environment issues. The research uses methodology that will be discussed in chapter four. Campbell maintains that these data provide a good deal of information about the type of student the institution should be recruiting.

The third task is strengthening academic programs, teaching, and student services. Campbell suggests that the institutional marketing committee carefully evaluate these activities, recognizing the critical role they play in fostering the institution's public image and in recruitment and retention efforts.

The fourth responsibility is assessment of the institution's promotional activities. Campbell asserts that colleges and universities often send out mixed messages, resulting in an ambiguous public image that confuses prospective students. This can lead to the loss of some of the best potential applicants and to the matriculation of students who would clearly be better off in another type of institution. Campbell suggests the institutional marketing committee spend time studying the actual benefits of college attendance:

Benefits speak more directly to the value of being in one place over another. Frequently, we neglect benefits in our discussions and messages, and consequently students must choose one institution over another as a result of a surface qualities—that is, institutional features alone (1980, p. 13).

The Advantages of a Marketing Committee

Campbell's institutional marketing committee is designed to increase campus awareness of institutional characteristics and resources and to help the office of admissions relay this information to prospective students and their parents. He views admissions personnel as facilitators: their role is to bring the message of what the campus does well to students and to attempt to match client needs with institutional resources.

Disadvantages of a Marketing Committee

Unlike the other models discussed in this section, the marketing committee model does not advocate that the committee exert direct coordinating control of recruitment or retention activities, although it may have such an effect in practice. Nor does it alter organizational structures to give these program areas a higher priority or greater voice in campus governance and decision-making. Thus, the Campbell model may be most useful for institutions where enrollment issues seem to be a future concern rather than a pressing problem.

In sum, the institutional marketing committee has an advisory role and probably has little influence in policy decisions. The model provides a forum for concerned parties on recruitment and enrollment issues, but it is not tied to campus decision centers in any way that might ultimately affect policies and decisions.

The Staff Coordinator: "Director of Enrollment Management"

Eugene Fram, Professor of Marketing at Rochester Institute of Technology, proposes that campuses create a new staff position to promote better coordination of campus marketing activities (Fram, 1975). Fram gave the position the title of "Director of

Marketing." However, as marketing carries a negative connotation, particularly in academic circles, the title of "Director of Enrollment Management" might be more appropriate.

Lack of Coordination among Programs

Fram identifies nine program areas that are involved in institutional marketing and promotional activities: admissions, public relations, retention, counseling, academic program development, alumni relations, job placement, institutional research, and development/fund raising. According to Fram, academic organizations—unlike industrial ones—do not assign a senior administrator to coordinate these activities. Fram's case-study work revealed that such program functions are usually independent of one another. Fram also found that supervisory responsibilities were generally divided, some assigned to the provost, and others assumed by the president.

Fram's case studies show that the absence of an administrative center to coordinate these interdependent programs often leads to organizational confusion and duplication of effort. On one campus, the publications department produced ineffectual promotional materials, largely because the department personnel did not understand the character of the institution's student body. At another, faculty instituted curricular changes without investigating their potential impact on recruitment efforts. And at a third college, development officers approached potential donors without any significant understanding of the college's educational mission, programs, or priorities.

Organizational Focus of the Office

To remedy these shortcomings, Fram proposes the creation of a new administrative staff position. Similar to the product manager in industrial organizations, the director of enrollment management would serve as an assistant to the president or provost and would be responsible for coordinating the nine previously cited program areas:

> *Line responsibility and authority for admissions and enrollment would be retained in its current organizational mode, with the major benefit of the director's work being an improvement of interdepartmental*

interface and overall consistency of purpose . . . the
director of marketing would examine the goals of every
department as they relate to the eight other areas of
marketing concern. Where goals are not congruent, the
director would seek changes or modifications (Fram,
1975, p. 6).

The director of enrollment management will have two major responsibilities: (1) coordination of interdependent program functions, such as admissions, public relations, and retention, and (2) development and implementation of an institutional marketing plan. Other activities also under the director's jurisdiction include disseminating enrollment-related data to various campus constituencies, preparing enrollment forecasts, and conducting market research.

Fram realizes that the director's job would be difficult. He recognizes that the director must have the stature and drive necessary to bring the various departments and functions together. Fram admits that the position would not be easy to fill "as there is no career path involved and one encounters the classical confrontation of having responsibility with little authority" (p. 9). He suggests that an experienced administrator who no longer desires a campus presidency might be interested in the position as a final step before retirement. Another candidate for the position might be a retired military officer or corporate executive.

Strengths in the "Director" Approach

Fram's model has several strong points. It recognizes a range of generally uncoordinated program functions that are, in fact, interdependent and linked to institutional efforts to maintain enrollments. It also attempts to provide an administrative center for these activities via the director of enrollment management position. Affiliated with either the office of the president or the provost, the director would be responsible for coordinating the full range of program functions that affect enrollment and public image. Fram's model acknowledges the critical role of institutional and market research, an area often neglected by many institutions. Finally, his model requires minor tinkering with the organizational chart: the director has a staff position.

Weakness in the "Director" Approach

Fram's model is not without its problems, however. The major disadvantage is that the position of director, as he envisions it, lacks sufficient integration into and stature within the organizational structure. Too much of the incumbent's influence and authority depends on the good will and cooperation of others. Without line responsibility, fiscal autonomy, and organizational rank, the position would be hobbled from the beginning. Fram admits that the industrial counterpart of this position, the product manager, has not worked well in all firms: "The major drawback has been the problem of having responsibility, for instance, to see that a certain number of production units are made but having no control over the production process" (p. 11).

Although a close working relationship with the president could ameliorate some of these problems, there is no escaping the fact that personality, persuasion, and trust—not administrative authority—are prerequisites to successful functioning in Fram's model. Successful administrators—particularly those who are agents for change and who are encumbered with the broad responsibilities described by Fram—need excellent personal skills coupled with administrative authority if they are to perform their jobs well.

The Matrix System: Sharing Resources

Enrollment difficulties that began in fall 1978 at California State University, Long Beach, led the institution to develop a "matrix" approach to enrollment management. Leonard Kreutner, Director of Admissions and Records, and Eric Godfrey, former Director of Financial Aid, were key participants. Their model, which does not require major changes in institutional structure, links enrollment-related functions under the jurisdiction of a senior administrator (Kreutner and Godfrey, 1980-81).

Elements in the Matrix Approach

The matrix model crosses administrative and academic lines to link enrollment activities according to program functions. Activities are grouped "according to their relative impact on some stage of the enrollment cycle, not according to the bureaucratic or administrative place they hold in the university" (p. 8). Kreutner and Godfrey identify four program areas or services: marketing, enrollment, retention, and research. Depending on their functions, campus offices and departments are assigned to one or another of the service areas. A senior vice president oversees the entire operation; at Long Beach it is the vice president for administration and staff coordination. This senior administrative "overseer" is authorized by the president to evaluate both academic and professional staff for their participation in the matrix system and to share these assessments with senior administrators from other departments.

The four program service areas are identified in Figure 3. Note that each area or module has a specific goal that does not overlap or duplicate the goal of other program modules. Furthermore, the activities of each module are limited so as not to overlap or duplicate the activities of other modules.

Role of Academic Departments

An important feature of the matrix model is that academic departments work closely with the admissions office. The departments have a major responsibility for contacting prospective students, developing recruitment literature, encouraging admitted students to enroll, and maintaining contact with students once they arrive on campus. Kreutner and Godfrey stress the importance of faculty participation in recruitment activities. "Faculty members are the most effective recruiters and it is much more difficult for a student to break ties with a department . . . than it is to leave a university" (p. 9). Records are an important tool in judging the success of the program. At Long Beach, Kreutner and Godfrey prepared enrollment management resource books, which charted departmental applications, acceptances, and yield rates.

Advantages of a Matrix Model

The matrix model, as described by Kreutner and Godfrey, has a number of advantages, particularly for large institutions. First, without initiating major changes in the organizational chart, the model provides a structure for diverse administrative and academic units to participate in enrollment management. The model links and coordinates various marketing, recruitment, and retention efforts according to program function; each module

Figure 3. Enrollment Management Modules at California State University, Long Beach

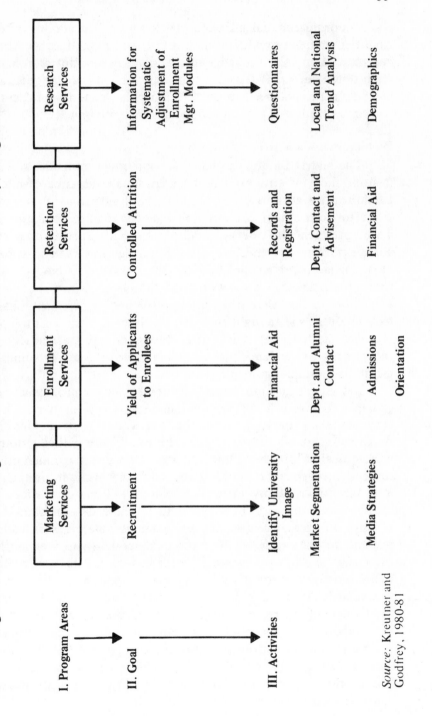

Source: Kreutner and Godfrey, 1980-81

has a coordinator and all are under a senior line administrator. And the model provides a vehicle for individual faculty members and academic departments to play a substantial role in recruitment efforts, thus encouraging student-faculty contact prior to matriculation and also defusing the tendency of faculty to blame enrollment problems on admissions personnel.

Problems with a Matrix Approach

The matrix model also has some potential problems. Because it stops short of structural reorganization, the absence of major administrative authority coupled with the limitations of cooperative effort can hinder coordination and goal attainment. Although a vice president does have overall responsibility for the program, administrative and academic units may assign low rank to enrollment management responsibilities. Other tasks may have greater priority, particularly if the "czar" of the system is not the senior administrator for that division. Faculty and department chairs may chafe at the thought of being involved in recruitment activities—in addition to their other responsibilities—particularly if the provost or academic vice president is not the senior administrator responsible for the program.

Indeed, structural issues can create major problems. For example, the fourth service module in this system is research, gathering data to feed back into the system (see Figure 3). As implemented at Long Beach, the use of the model requires a great deal of data including applicant characteristics, marketing surveys, departmental yield rates, and retention information. Yet, the Office of Institutional Research at Long Beach reports to the academic vice president and is charged with gathering a range of financial, faculty, and student data, few of which respond to the needs of the matrix components. Consequently, the Office of Admissions and Records had to hire its own specialist to conduct enrollment management research. In our interviews, officials at Long Beach agreed that major problems such as this can only be resolved through structural change.

Still, the matrix model does encourage diverse departments to participate in enrollment management activities, thus promoting faculty and administrative involvement in recruitment and retention efforts. Judging from the experience at Long Beach, the model represents a viable alternative to more radical structural reorganization.

The Enrollment Management Division

The model that requires the most restructuring of the existing organizational chart is the enrollment management division model proposed by William L. Caren and Frank R. Kemerer, Dean of Admissions and former Director of Enrollment Management, respectively, at the State University of New York (SUNY) College of Arts and Science at Geneseo. They suggest that successful enrollment management requires major organizational change: "We subscribe to the view expressed by Katz and Kahn that to change the organization, *one needs to change the organization"* (Caren and Kemerer, 1979, p. 180). Katz and Kahn, organizational sociologists, express this sentiment another way:

> *If we are really dealing with an organizational or system variable, its manipulation will involve the entire organization. To achieve organizational change, we have to deal with system variables. Individual or group change applies only to specific points in organizational space, and is more likely to be vitiated by the enduring systemic properties than to change them (1966, p. 427).*

Caren and Kemerer propose creating a new position known as the "Vice President for Institutional Advancement" (VPIA). Rather than simply an appendage to the existing organization, this vice president would have full responsibility for offices and activities directly related to enrollment management and institutional advancement. Figure 4 illustrates the organizational chart for a college or university with an enrollment ranging from 5,000 to 10,000 students.

Advantages of Reorganization

Caren and Kemerer assert that the advantages of this model are numerous. First and foremost, the vice president for institutional advancement is sufficiently integrated into the decision-

Figure 4. Caren and Kemerer's VPIA Model

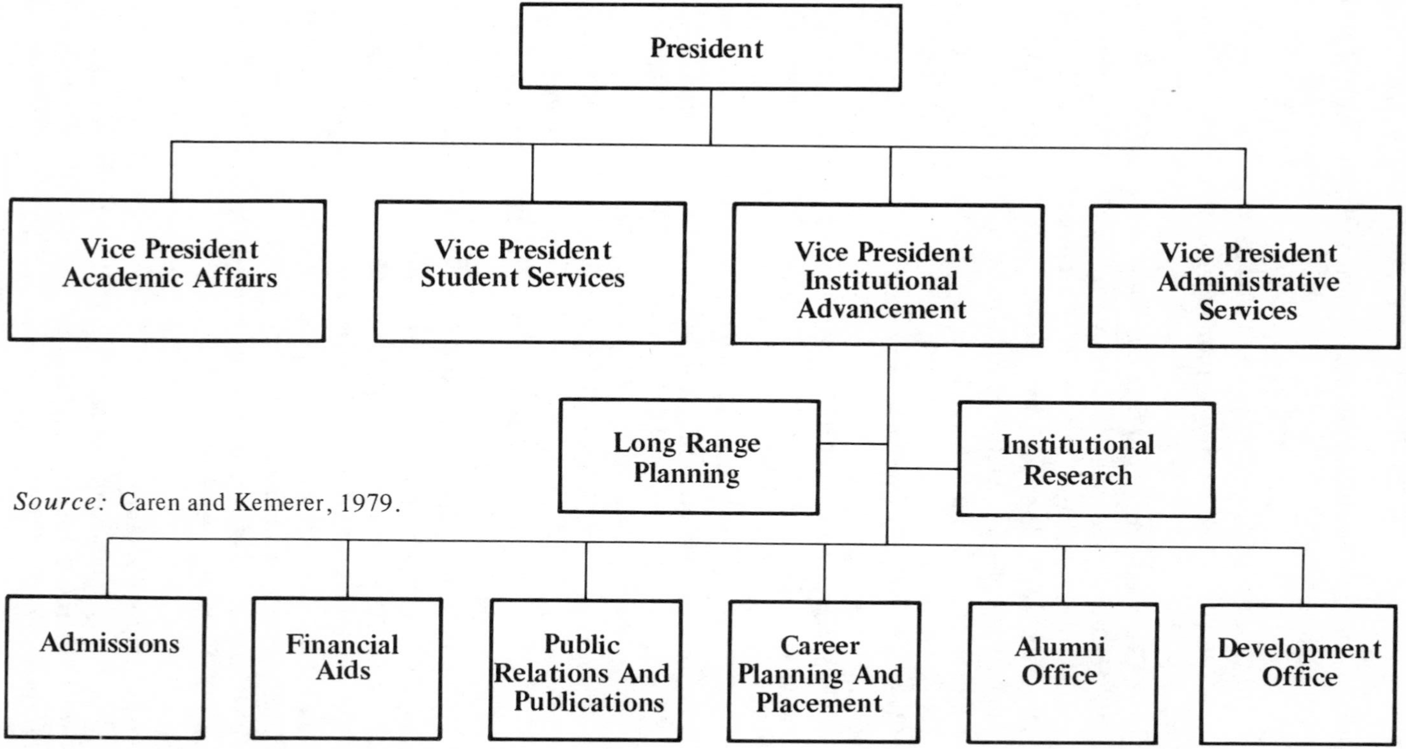

Source: Caren and Kemerer, 1979.

and policy-making structure to ensure that enrollment management concerns receive adequate administrative attention.

> *By advocating this model we are espousing a basic principle of organizational theory: form must follow function; the goals of the organization should determine how its resources are utilized. . . . Cooperative planning and decision-making in support of a coherent plan for institutional advancement are often compromised by conflicting allegiances, incongruent priorities, and bureaucratic isolation (Caren and Kemerer, 1979, p. 182).*

Caren and Kemerer cite several examples of organizational conflict affecting enrollment management. An institutional research office that reports to an academic officer tends to reflect the concerns of that division by emphasizing academic planning data and neglecting market research. Alumni and publication offices are often unaware of recruitment efforts because they respond to different priorities. The requests of prospective students for career development information may go unanswered because that office is in another division.

As a line administrator, the vice president for institutional advancement has sufficient authority to secure cooperation from administrative colleagues and other administrative units. Both the planning and institutional research offices would be under the vice president, thus centralizing and enhancing the dissemination of important data. The holder of the new position would have access to important policy forums and could see that institutional research was used in program development, resource allocation, and strategic planning. Caren and Kemerer claim that creating the VPIA position would "make a measured commitment to institutional advancement, provide greater visibility for the various marketing functions . . . and build a better measure of accountability" (p. 182).

Potential Problems with Reorganization
The VPIA model is not without its problems. First, many institutions cannot—or perhaps should not—attempt major structural changes. A modest restructuring is represented by the stu-

dent planning division established at Bradley University. (See chapter five for details.) Second, during a period of retrenchment, institutions will have a hard time justifying yet another administrative unit and additional staff. Even where retrenchment is not a problem, the president may be reluctant to traumatize the administration by initiating major organizational changes, particularly if personnel have been in place for a number of years. Furthermore, major structural change, while promising significant long-term benefits, is not without some sizeable short-term costs: anticipated long-term benefits must be assessed against short-term instability. In spite of these problems, however, Caren and Kemerer believe that "the exigencies of institutional enrollment problems are sufficiently great in many colleges and universities to warrant the creation of a new executive line position at the vice president level" (p. 180).

Assessment of the Four Models

We said earlier that successful enrollment management requires some sort of change in the organizational status quo. Each of the models previously described represents one organizational approach to integrating enrollment management into institutional decision- and policy-making. Some models require little restructuring; others involve a major overhaul of the organizational chart.

Table 4 compares the major characteristics of each approach. Each is designed to improve data acquisition and dissemination, as well as improve communications and understanding about the campus enrollment problems. Three of the four go a step further to address problems of coordinating recruiting and retention activities.

Recent Changes in Administrative Organization: Our Survey Results

In the sections above we outlined reorganizations that institutions might want to consider. But what have they actually done? Have many institutions initiated structural changes to respond to the demographic and financial challenges of the 1980s? The 1981

Table 4: Comparison of Four Enrollment Management Models

Model	Major Goals and Activities	Personnel	Authority	Structural Changes
Institutional Marketing Committee (Campbell 1980)	Assess and communicate	Committee structure involves mostly administrators but includes some faculty.	Little—committee serves in an advisory capacity.	None—committee has an advisory role, may be an ad hoc institutional response.
Staff Coordinator (Fran 1975)	Coordinate programs that affect enrollment and develop market plan.	Staff person organizationally placed as a special assistant to the provost or president.	Little—position lacks line authority and resources. Influence depends upon persuasion and good will.	Minor—staff appointment that has little impact on organization.
Matrix Model (Kreutner and Godfrey 1980-81)	Link enrollment activities according to program function without regard for divisional structure.	Senior line administrator who is authorized to evaluate personnel in other divisions.	Assigned by the president but perhaps superseded by divisional powers.	Minor—model attempts to link activities and offices without major structural changes.
Enrollment Management Division (Caren and Kemerer 1980)	Coordinate and control all activities affecting enrollment.	Senior line administrator.	Potentially high.	Significant—program function areas formally assigned to a line administrator.

National Enrollment Survey indicates that half of the U.S. colleges and universities have undergone administrative reorganization since 1976. According to the institutions' presidents, roughly one-third of the reorganizations were "major" changes; the rest were "some" or "minor" changes. AASCU institutions and private four-year colleges more than others reported major administrative reorganization during the past five years.

Although reorganization may not have been explicitly linked to enrollment concerns, the survey data reveal that the admissions office and the student affairs office—major components of enrollment activities—were the areas most likely to be involved in the administrative change (Table 5). Indeed, institutions that seem most likely to experience enrollment problems in the 1980s—private four-year colleges and AASCU schools—were most likely to report changes in admissions and student affairs.

The survey of admissions officers reveals that nearly one-third now report to a different office than they did five years ago. Who ends up with line responsibility for the admissions office? Open-ended responses from our surveys reveal that most of the restructuring has moved admissions away from academic affairs and towards the president or the vice president for student affairs. Some admissions directors say they now report to a planning and development office. One respondent's office had been shifted three times in the past five years—from the president's office to student affairs, then to academic affairs, and finally to educational planning!

The realignment of the admissions office on many campuses suggests that administrators are struggling to halt or slow declining enrollments. The models discussed in this chapter should help campus officials see a range of enrollment management possibilities, any or all of which might be appropriate for an individual campus.

Summary

It is both fruitless and unfair to saddle the office of admissions with major responsibility for successful student recruitment and retention. Successful enrollment management is really everyone's responsibility. Campuses must promote better understanding

Table 5: Campuses Experiencing Administrative Reorganization, 1976-1981
(percentage of presidents responding)

Survey Question	Public Research Univ.	AASCU Inst.	Private 2-Year Coll.	Private Univ.	Private 4-Year Coll.	Private 2-Year Coll.	All Inst.
1. Yes, We Have Experienced Reorganization,	50	61	51	31	55	33	51
2. Areas Affected by Reorganization							
Academic Affairs	37	37	36	23	32	11	31
Admissions	37	36	25	31	47	33	35
Financial Affairs	17	30	18	15	34	22	25
Student Affairs	27	43	39	15	33	22	33

43

of enrollment issues and improve coordination of recruitment and retention efforts. We have presented four possible models of organizing these efforts based on the literature. Each model has distinct advantages and disadvantages and may help at some institutions but not at others. In the next chapter we look at another managerial task: how to help the office of admissions function more effectively and efficiently.

CHAPTER 3
Revitalizing the Office
of Admissions

We have argued that enrollment management encompasses a good deal more than student recruitment. But let us not overstate the case. Student recruitment is central to successful enrollment management. The office of admissions must operate as efficiently and effectively as possible. We have already noted that most offices of admissions are not directly linked to top administrative and faculty decision-making. Our concern now is with the *internal* operations of offices of admissions. How adequate are existing staffing patterns? To what extent are admissions personnel happy in their work? How might the office of admissions be strengthened? This chapter considers these questions.

Personnel Issues

Admissions personnel are institutional road-runners—they keep information about the campus flowing to high school and community college counselors. They are constantly looking for prospective students. Because they perform a low-visibility function and often spend most of their professional time away from the campus, admissions personnel are sometimes taken for granted. Recent research reveals that the job concerns of admissions personnel should not be overlooked by top administrators. Let us examine some of these personnel issues more closely.

A Profile of the Director of Admissions
The director of admissions is an administrative position in transition. At some institutions the registrar serves as the director of admissions. Elsewhere, particularly on smaller campuses, the director of admissions may supervise the financial aid office.

However, the growing specialization in all three areas—recruitment, records, and financial aid—has tended to separate these offices. The administrators who head them are no longer simply student affairs generalists but professionals in their own right. As noted in the previous chapter, specialization has tended to exacerbate the breakdown in communication among offices concerned with enrollment management.

Marginal Status. Most directors of admissions do not have academic rank and are not eligible for tenure. A recent National Salary and Compensation Study commissioned by the National Association of College Admissions Counselors (NACAC) shows that slightly over one-quarter of the directors of admissions at public institutions hold academic rank. For private institutions, the percentage varies from 27 percent at two-year institutions to 16 percent at universities (Chapman and Johnson, 1981, p. 20).

Classified for the most part as middle-level administrators, some admissions directors feel like second-class citizens. As one director told us, "It's ironic. Every time I go before the faculty senate, I feel like a hired hand. Yet they depend upon me to generate enough students to save their jobs!" Organizationally, the absence of faculty rank reinforces the remoteness of the director of admissions from the centers of decision-making.

High Turnover. Our National Enrollment Survey shows that turnover among admissions directors is high. Fifty percent of the admissions directors responding served four years or less. Private four-year and two-year institutions have the most turnover, public and private universities the least. The pattern at AASCU institutions is mixed. Twenty-eight percent of AASCU admissions directors say they are new to their jobs, serving only one or two years; 33 percent have served between three and seven years; the remainder have served in their positions over eight years. When viewed regionally, the turnover is largest in the Northeast and Midwest, where enrollment problems have been the most pronounced. Admissions directors report the turnover of their immediate predecessor was also high, with almost 60 percent having served four years or less.

Mixed Job Satisfaction. The 1981 NACAC salary and compensation survey included some questions about job satisfaction. The results show that admissions directors are relatively happy with their jobs (Figure 5). Despite high turnover, four out of

Figure 5. Career Paths of Directors of Admissions
(percentages)

Patterns of Entry into Admissions

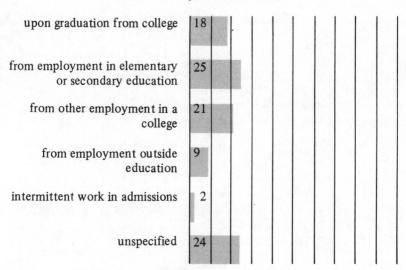

upon graduation from college	18
from employment in elementary or secondary education	25
from other employment in a college	21
from employment outside education	9
intermittent work in admissions	2
unspecified	24

Who Serves as Director

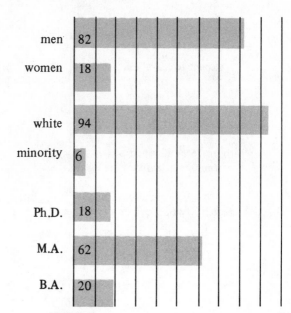

men	82
women	18
white	94
minority	6
Ph.D.	18
M.A.	62
B.A.	20

Figure 5. (con't) Career Paths of Directors of Admissions

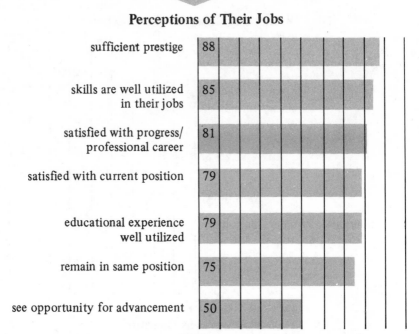

Perceptions of Their Jobs

sufficient prestige	88
skills are well utilized in their jobs	85
satisfied with progress/ professional career	81
satisfied with current position	79
educational experience well utilized	79
remain in same position	75
see opportunity for advancement	50

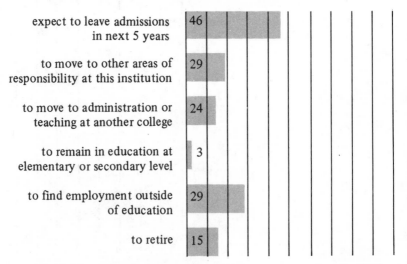

Future Career Paths

expect to leave admissions in next 5 years	46
to move to other areas of responsibility at this institution	29
to move to administration or teaching at another college	24
to remain in education at elementary or secondary level	3
to find employment outside of education	29
to retire	15

Source: NACAC 1980-81 Survey by David Chapman & Sandra Urbach, 1982

every five report satisfaction in their professional career and are "very" to "extremely" satisfied with their current position. Yet, *nearly half* see little opportunity for advancement and 46 percent expect to leave the admissions field within the next five years! Of those leaving, 53 percent expect to move to other areas of postsecondary education, while almost one-third hope to pursue opportunities outside of education. The desire to leave is highest among women and minorities. Roughly 58 percent of the women and 53 percent of minority officers expect to leave admissions work within five years.

Viewed by type of institution, the data show that admissions directors at universities are most pleased with their current employment—86 percent saying very or extremely pleased as compared with 79 percent at two-year campuses and 76 percent at four-year. Likewise, university admissions directors see more advancement opportunities than their counterparts at two- and four-year institutions. But nearly half the directors at four-year campuses say their duties take up too much of their personal time as compared with 33 percent at universities and 28 percent at two-year campuses. Viewed regionally, the data show job satisfaction is strongest in the Southwest (86 percent) and weakest in the Northeast (76 percent). Prospects for advancement are felt more strongly in the Southwest (61 percent) than in the Northeast and Northwest (47 percent for each).

Difficulty of Career Ladder Progression. The fact that most admissions directors are relatively happy with their jobs suggests that their plans to leave are more related to a desire for career advancement than frustration on the job. Still, the NACAC researchers find the responses disturbing, for admissions personnel are unlikely to realize the job mobility they expect.

Two factors work against interdepartmental mobility. First, admissions officers typically do not hold a doctorate, increasingly a necessity for top administrative positions in higher education. Second, as many colleges face the need to stabilize or even reduce the number of faculty, more faculty are likely to see college administration as a viable alternative for themselves. Admissions directors may be in increasing competition with faculty for the other administrative positions that are available (Chapman and Urbach, 1982, p. 25).

The absence of a career ladder for admissions directors, then, poses a threat to future job satisfaction. At the same time, increasing pressure from top-level administrators and faculty for more effective recruiting may very well erode the present high levels of job satisfaction. At many institutions, admissions directors may come to have something in common with athletic coaches—job security is a function of a successful season.

A Profile of the Admissions Counselor

Admissions is generally viewed as an entry-level occupation. No specialized training is necessary for admissions work. Admissions counselors spend most of their time traveling or interviewing prospective students on campus. What has to be learned is learned on the job. As a result, many become counselors right after graduation from college (note patterns of entry of directors of admissions in Figure 5). As noted later, this lack of training may work to the disadvantage of the institution, for effective student recruiting and retention increasingly are becoming technical enterprises that require sophisticated knowledge of information gathering and processing, marketing principles, and resource management.

Low Salaries. Research by the NACAC shows the salary levels of admissions counselors to be quite low (Chapman and Urbach, 1982). For example, the mean counselor's salary in 1981 was $13,697. This compares with $20,206 for associate directors and $24,852 for admissions directors. All are twelve-month positions. NACAC salary data also show that the number of minority counselors is much higher at public than at private colleges, although those at private colleges tend to earn more; men outnumber women by nearly three to one at the director level but women outnumber men at the counselor level; men have substantially higher salaries at both public and private institutions than women holding similar jobs; and admissions personnel at all ranks earn more in public colleges than at private institutions.

High Turnover Rates. Not surprisingly, turnover is high for admissions counselors, especially among women and minorities and at private colleges where counselors usually serve little more than two years before moving on. Research focused on NACAC membership only and conducted by Urbach and Chapman (1982) shows that nearly half of admissions counselors responding are only somewhat or not at all satisfied with their jobs and see no opportunity for future advancement. A whopping 90 percent expect to leave admissions within the next five years, over half for positions outside of education. The percentages are somewhat less dramatic for assistant and associate directors. Roughly 30 percent of both groups are only somewhat or not at all satisfied with their jobs. Sixty-two percent of the assistant directors plan to leave admissions within five years; 54 percent of the associate directors plan to do so. Even though this research centers on NACAC membership only and overrepresents private four-year colleges, one senses that low morale may be pervasive among junior staff.

Many admissions counselors, of course, do stay with admissions, working up through the ranks. Research shows that associate directors of admissions at both public and private colleges tend to have been at their current institution longer than the admissions directors (Chapman and Urbach, 1982). Either they chose not to be considered for the top job or were passed over. In any case, the director of admissions and other administrators cannot ignore the issue of job satisfaction or career options for junior staff.

Staffing the Office of Admissions

The 1981 National Enrollment Survey offers some interesting facts about admission personnel. How do various types of institutions compare with respect to the numbers of full-time professional staff assigned to the admissions office? As noted in Table 6, there are dramatic differences among types of institutions. Because of their larger size, universities require more professional staff members to carry out recruiting and admissions processing functions. The largest staffs are located at private universities, which conduct extensive out-of-state recruitment. The most significant findings, however, involve the size of the staff at AASCU and private four-year institutions. Though larger, AASCU institutions lag behind their private sector counterparts in staff size. One suspects that as public institutions move more aggressively into school-by-school recruiting in the future, the disparity may lessen. Until recently, these institutions were growing and did not have to engage in heavy off-campus recruiting to maintain enrollments. Whether the method adopted by private two-year institutions (with over 65 percent reporting four or five staff members assigned to freshmen admissions) will be the wave of the future remains to be seen. Insofar as undergraduate and transfer admissions staffs are concerned, survey results show most institutions assign only one or two full-time professional staff to these areas. (Data not shown in Table 6).

The Need for Staff Development

Rapid turnover in the office of admissions, especially at the lower ranks, has both benefits and drawbacks. One benefit may be lower personnel costs. If an institution has a training program that is self-administered or can be administered with minimal supervision by the director or associate director, then rapid turnover may be manageable.

There are, however, major drawbacks. One may be low morale. The lack of job satisfaction and the desire to find another job expressed by many junior staffers may get in the way of effective job performance. A second major drawback is the retarding effect turnover has on the development of knowledge and skills. Given the absence of degree and credentialing programs for admissions officers, entry-level personnel come to the job unprepared. In-service training takes time. Constantly having to retrain new employees also costs money.

A Professional Development Program

It may be advantageous to lower the turnover of admissions personnel, and one way to accomplish this is by addressing their job concerns. One tactic, even in small offices of only three or four professionals, is to develop a professional development program to upgrade skills and insights. Both of the national admissions officers associations—NACAC and AACRAO—are planning future preservice programs to address these needs. Most campuses offer courses in counseling, assessment, management information systems, computers, communications, and marketing, which, in combination with publications and training workshops

Table 6: Size of Professional Freshman Admissions Staff
(percentage of admissions directors responding)

Office Size	Public Research Univ.	AASCU Inst.	Public 2-Year Coll.	Private Univ.	Private 4-Year Coll.	Private 2-Year Coll.	All Inst.
One Staff Member	3	13	**31**	0	3	0	14
Two Staff Members	13	**20**	**25**	0	8	0	**15**
Three Staff Members	3	**25**	13	0	**17**	**22**	**16**
Four Staff Members	**15**	12	4	0	**20**	**33**	14
Five Staff Members	13	9	2	8	**21**	**33**	13
Six Staff Members	**18**	4	4	**15**	14	0	8
Seven or More	**26**	8	6	**70**	14	11	12

Numbers in boldface indicate a response of 15 percent or more.

the professional associations and their local affiliates now offer, could be useful in upgrading the skills of admissions personnel. Indeed, many academic departments currently offer professional development in-service training programs to business and industry.

Developing a Career Ladder

A career ladder program designed to offer admissions personnel an opportunity for professional advancement could go a long way to improve the quality, efficiency, and effectiveness of admissions personnel and at the same time address the issue of career options and advancement.

In order for a career ladder to work most effectively, staffing should be differentiated in the office of admissions. Implementing a differentiated staffing structure involves grouping tasks together to form specialized positions, such as transfer admissions counselor, graduate admissions coordinator, communications coordinator, and enrollment research director. Each position requires certain professional skills and insights. Employees who through in-service training have achieved the necessary qualifications would be eligible for these positions. Motivated and talented counselors could advance to jobs requiring greater responsibility and expertise until they attain senior positions. Not only does the employee benefit by seeing a well-marked road for professional advancement ahead, the office of admissions benefits by having better trained staff members.

Campus administrators need to be concerned about the career aspirations of admissions directors. A career ladder could be developed within an entire student affairs division by establishing links among various positions and identifying the necessary prerequisites for promotion. By linking positions together through a career ladder program augmented by a professional development program, institutions perhaps could pave the way for the admissions director to advance to a higher level position in logical stair-step manner.

Personnel Evaluation

Some people do not belong in admissions. A well-developed staff evaluation program can identify these persons objectively, as well as pinpoint weaknesses and strengths for all professionals.

Evaluation criteria and techniques are sometimes spelled out in collective bargaining agreements, state law, and institutional policies. Where this is not the case, professionals in the office of admissions should work together to establish them. Assessment *criteria* grow out of departmental objectives and job descriptions; assessment *techniques* must be carefully selected to yield information relevant to the criteria. Assessment techniques usually vary and might include self-appraisals, evaluation by a superior, ratings by prospective students or high school counselors or both, and on-site visits by outside consultants.

Regardless of *how* an evaluation is made, what is important is that an evaluation occur! Evaluation provides information useful for personnel decisions, enables professional development activities to be more carefully targeted to employee needs, and furnishes the necessary documentation for substantiating negative decisions.

Adequate Resources for Admissions

Our 1981 National Enrollment Survey asked admissions directors whether various recruitment-related activities have increased since 1975. Forty-three percent of the admissions directors responding report budget increases above inflation levels from 1975 to 1980; 23 percent report staff increases above replacement. Institutions differ significantly by type, however. Private colleges and universities increased staff and particularly budget at a greater rate than public institutions. About 11 percent of the directors of admissions indicate they plan to increase their budgets. For AASCU respondents, the percentages are 13 percent and 17 percent, respectively.

Frankly we were surprised to learn that so few respondents foresee increasing the operating budget of the office of admissions. Effective recruitment costs money. Obviously, at a time of shrinking resources, commitment from top administrators must be particularly strong to shift more dollars to enrollment management. Doing so may be a critical step toward institutional vitality.

Without resources, the office of admissions is hobbled from the beginning. As noted earlier, salary levels for admissions officers are comparatively low, thus contributing to employee turnover.

Some campuses lack the personnel to mount an effective recruiting program. For example, a task force at North Texas State University (NTSU), an institution of 17,500 students in the Dallas-Ft. Worth metroplex, was surprised to find only three admissions officers employed by the university. Saddled with extensive admissions processing duties, they could mount only a limited recruitment program across the state. As a result, relationships with high school counselors—many of them North Texas graduates—were neglected. Most off-campus recruiting focused on cattle call-like college nights and fairs. Despite the fact that the transfer pool was the largest source of new students, there was no one at North Texas to coordinate transfer recruiting. Graduate student recruitment was left to individual schools and departments—with mixed results. Nor was there adequate staffing to coordinate university recruitment literature or mount a focused minority recruitment program.

This situation, we fear, is typical of many campuses, both public and private. In a period of retrenchment it is difficult to shift resources away from the other areas to admissions. Yet without sufficient resources, effective recruiting cannot occur. Fortunately, a new administration at North Texas State made the difficult decision to increase staffing in the office of admissions despite a period of financial stress. The new administration also opted to work toward the implementation of other task force recommendations—some of them very expensive—to improve the flow of students into and through the institution. Within a year, the university experienced a turnaround. Enrollees increased by nearly 10 percent in the fall of 1982, and the dormitories were unable to accommodate all of the students requesting housing.

Revitalizing Admissions: The SUNY-Geneseo Case Study

The SUNY College of Arts and Science at Geneseo confronted this problem in the mid-1970s when the college experienced an unexpected shortfall of 500 students.

Dimensions of Geneseo's Problem

A close look at some trend data should have convinced administrators that something was wrong. In 1971, the campus granted admission to about 46 percent of the total number of freshman applicants. But by 1975, the proportion of applicants admitted had dramatically increased to 84 percent. This increase was necessary in order to maintain a freshman class of about 1,200 students. As early as 1973 the figures showed that the "yield" of enrolled students from those being granted admission had declined significantly. Apparently, more and more students were choosing the college as a back-up institution. Had this fact been realized earlier, the college could have made a concerted effort to assess the situation and develop effective counteraction. As it was, the kind of rational approach to effective recruitment suggested in the next chapter had ceased to be a viable option.

What was particularly disturbing about the shortfall was that the number of high school graduates in New York State continued to increase during this period. No significant *decrease* was expected until the end of the decade. If Geneseo was already experiencing declines in the 1970s, what would happen in the 1980s? Equally disturbing was the financial collapse of New York City in 1975 that ushered in a period of financial cutbacks by the State government, and consequently, the SUNY system. From 1975 to 1977, a total of 2,500 positions were eliminated from SUNY's budget. Could Geneseo recoup its loses in sufficient time to avoid having to retrench?

Actions to Solve the Problem

Wishing to give new life to student recruitment, the campus president placed the office of admissions together with several other offices related to student recruitment in a special unit supervised by his executive assistant. Although an extensive list of remedial actions were proposed, only low-cost activities were deemed feasible.

It became immediately clear that the college was not visiting a large number of high schools from which it received applicants. It was also clear that the material about the college in the files of high school counselors was sparse and dated. The decision was made to begin a modest publications program and to increase school-by-school recruiting. Departmental budgets helped some with the publications effort, but there simply was no money for hiring more recruiters.

Faced with this situation, the executive assistant and the director of admissions developed several programs to increase the size of the professional recruitment staff without spending large amounts of money. The first was the Adjunct Recruiter Program. It drew on the services of those administrators at the college who had previously had some admissions office experience. Seven administrators were released from regular duties for one or two weeks to help with recruitment. The seven participated in a special training and updating program before leaving the campus. The adjunct recruiters usually visited schools in their hometown area or in regions of the state where they had ties.

The second activity was the Admissions Internship Program. Two graduates of the college were selected by a screening committee to work in the admissions office. They were expected to function as full-fledged admissions officers under the supervision of the director of admissions. Each was paid a stipend, given room and board at campus housing, and an opportunity for tuition-free graduate study at a nearby institution. This program provided a much-needed increase in full-time admissions staffing at low cost. At the same time, it offered those interested in student affairs work an opportunity to gain experience.

A Student Volunteer Admissions Program was also developed. The 125 volunteers, primarily freshmen and sophomores, agreed to meet with interested high school students over vacation breaks in their hometown communities to acquaint them with campus life. The volunteers participated in a special training program and then were supplied with appropriate materials along with the names and addresses of students who had either applied or expressed some interest in the college. Letters were also sent to high schools in their communities indicating the volunteers would be available to meet with interested students. Later, an Alumni Volunteer Admissions Program modeled along the same lines was developed.

The Payoff: Increased Enrollments from Low-Cost Activities

These low-cost programs enabled the office of admissions to expand the size of its professional staff, quadruple off-campus recruitment, and do a much better job of follow-up with interested students and applicants. At present, the college, which has an enrollment of 5,000 students and recruits only in New York

State, has a recruiting staff consisting of four full-time recruiters, one full-time student intern, and ten adjunct recruiters in addition to the director of admissions. Fall recruitment typically involves over 500 visits to high schools and community colleges.

The increased personal contact between potential students and college personnel was instrumental in reversing the shortfall. Between 1978 and 1981, applications for admissions jumped 54 percent. The college now needs to admit fewer than half its applicants to meet its new student enrollment goals. According to a recent study, less than 10 percent of four-year public and private colleges in the United States can make this claim (Hartlett and Feldmesser, 1980). At the same time, the quality of the applicants, as reflected in their high school averages and aptitude test scores, has increased significantly and this has had a positive effect on retention. Nearly 80 percent of the freshman class now return as sophomores. In 1978, the figure was 71 percent. What is most startling about the reversal is that it has occurred in a period of declining numbers of high school graduates in New York State. Over a period of several years, Geneseo went from having one of the worst student recruitment records in the SUNY system to having one of the best—without lowering standards or dramatically changing campus mission and programs.

Using a shortcut to obtain new personnel, of course, did not negate the need for additional funds at Geneseo. Considerable amounts of money were shifted from other areas to underwrite the costs of undertaking new recruiting and admissions procedures and techniques. There simply is no way to be effective in student recruitment without spending money. We believe one of the best investments would be for a college to underwrite the costs of a professional development program for admissions staff members as described in the previous section.

Other Improvement Strategies

Let us now examine two other suggestions for revitalizing admissions—breaking the paperwork logjam and building faculty involvement in admissions.

Speeding Up the Paperwork Flow

Our computer age has ushered in a variety of labor-saving devices designed to increase efficiency by speeding up the paperwork. Yet many organizations, including institutions of higher education, are slow to adopt new ways of doing business. The special task force established at North Texas State University noted that North Texas State continues to register students the old fashioned way—in person and by hand. Since North Texas State is largely a commuter institution, many students would prefer to register by mail or phone. They would also like to be billed by mail and arrange course changes via mail or phone.

To rectify these problems as well as to keep better track of students generally, the North Texas State task force recommended adoption of a computerized integrated student information system. Such a system would accommodate the computing needs of a large portion of the NTSU administrative community, could provide hard-to-get information about admissions and academic records, and would free faculty for advising. What is particularly attractive about such a system is its ability to provide instantaneous data about a particular student at any point from the initial recruiting contact to alumnus status. Through such data, the university would be better able to direct individual attention to student needs. For example, the university could be alerted when a student is slow to complete an application, fails to return an assessment instrument, does not take advantage of early registration, is in academic difficulty, fails to re-enroll over the summer, and so on. Appropriate letters and phone calls can be initiated much more easily than would be the case with a manual system. The possibilities for improved student admission and retention seem endless.

Most admissions personnel can probably identify at least a dozen ways to speed up the flow of paperwork. Virtually every institution can benefit from the use of word processing equipment, which increases productivity and also reduces clerical costs. Differentiated staffing can help speed paperwork. An audit of all forms currently used in recruitment and admissions could eliminate redundancy and requests for irrelevant information. We urge that institutions take the time to review current practices—the sooner, the better.

Establishing Links with the Faculty

As we noted in chapter two, successful enrollment management requires substantial faculty participation. In our survey, 67 percent of campus presidents agreed that admissions policies at their institutions have been the topic of serious discussion among faculty. The percentage was lowest at two-year public institutions (45 percent) and highest at private universities and two-year institutions (92 and 100 percent, respectively). For AASCU institutions, the figure was 69 percent.

Eighty-one percent of campus presidents also agree that their faculty have displayed increased interest in recruiting issues and are more willing to help recruit students. The percentage of agreement was similar at all types of institutions, except public universities (64 percent).

Building Faculty Awareness. On some campuses, it may take considerable time to overcome faculty ignorance and apathy about campus enrollment problems. At Bradley University, where effective enrollment management has been going on for some time, faculty disinterest and apathy remain a serious impediment, particularly in terms of retention strategies. The Marketing Task Force at the SUNY College of Arts and Science at Potsdam recommended that the results of enrollment research studies be highlighted in the college newspaper to overcome faculty ignorance and apathy. At SUNY-Geneseo, this technique, coupled with a two-day off-campus retreat to which key faculty members, administrators, and students were invited, was used to alert the campus to the implications of the 1977 student shortfall. Highlights of the reports presented at the retreat were featured in the campus newspaper, followed by discussion of enrollment problems at a faculty meeting chaired by the president.

Efforts such as these will help overcome faculty apathy and disinterest. But improving faculty awareness is not enough. Faculty must be actively involved in enrollment management activities. Research conducted by Old Dominion University in Norfolk shows that faculty contact with potential students has a significant impact on college choice. In our national enrollment survey, 42 percent of the presidents agreed with the statement "Faculty have been heavily involved in developing strategies to cope with enrollment concerns."

A Liaison System for Faculty Involvement. Probably the most effective avenue for faculty involvement is through academic departments. Two of our case-study institutions, SUNY-Geneseo and California State University at Long Beach, developed formal programs to link academic departments with the office of admissions. With the approval of the president and vice president for academic affairs, both set up a liaison system whereby each academic department had a representative who served as the liaison with the office of admissions. California State at Long Beach assembled an Enrollment Management Resource Book for each department containing that department's admissions history, including number of applicants, number of admissions, and yield ratios. This information was discussed with each department. Needless to say, most faculty members had never seen this information before and in some cases were shocked to see serious erosion in the figures.

Department liaisons at SUNY-Geneseo were constantly fed admissions data to share with colleagues. They were asked to set up meetings with prospective students, to contact interested students by mail or phone, to assist with efforts to get outstanding department members into high schools and community colleges as guest lecturers, and to take the initiative in developing attractive departmental literature. The office of admissions provided the names and addresses of students, offered its word processing equipment for correspondence, and in some cases helped fund the costs of developing new literature.

At both institutions, California State University at Long Beach and SUNY-Geneseo, the level of faculty interest and cooperation varied from department to department. Some departments took the liaison system seriously and selected very capable representatives. In many cases, the department chairperson opted to serve as liaison. Some departments made a concerted effort to work with the admissions and academic affairs offices to develop articulation agreements with their counterparts in community colleges. A few even offered to have faculty members travel with college recruiters to promote the department. Many were surprised to find their counterparts in high schools and community colleges eager to host a guest lecture or performance.

A few departments did not cooperate as extensively as they might have. Some, of course, did not feel the need in light of their high enrollments. But others did not get going even though they were in obvious enrollment difficulty. At California State University at Long Beach, the initial success convinced others to climb aboard. Of the thirteen departments that participated in the liaison system the first year, twelve had yield increases larger than that for the university as a whole. At SUNY-Geneseo, a letter from the president to uncooperative departments with enrollment troubles pointed out that in an era of retrenchment, those departments with falling enrollments would likely be the first to suffer staffing cutbacks. The letter was sufficient to prod even the most reluctant to an uncharacteristically high level of cooperation.

A Liaison System for Graduate Recruiting. Most graduate programs are handled on the department or school level, and while the departments may want to improve student recruitment they usually do not know how. In the public sector, institutions often receive more money through the formula funding system for master's and doctoral degree students. Since this is the case, it could be argued that graduate student recruitment should be more centralized. For example, Old Dominion University has a separate office for graduate admissions in the Division of Enrollment Services to coordinate research and recruiting of graduate students. Where centralization is not feasible, however, a liaison system could foster more tutored student recruitment at the graduate level.

An Effective Liaison System. A departmental liaison system can be effective in getting faculty members involved in recruitment. But merely setting one up is no guarantee of success. Some prerequisites for successful implementation include the following:

• Determine ahead of time whether such a system is necessary and if so how it is to function.

• Have the means to gather enrollment data at the departmental level and be willing to share it even though interdepartmental rivalry will inevitably increase.

• Secure the full backing of the president and especially the vice president of academic affairs; they may have to do some arm-twisting to get things moving in some departments.

• Offer support services to departments that usually do not have sufficient funds to underwrite travel expenses, phone calls, printing of new literature, and even postage.

• Appoint someone in the office of admissions to coordinate the liaison system so that it does not languish.

In addition to a department liaison system, a faculty admissions committee can help communicate admissions-related matters to the faculty governance body. Many campuses already have such committees. In the past, they were generally inactive, meeting only twice a year to review admissions standards. The present pressure to maintain enrollments gives such committees a new lease on life. They can serve as a sounding board for new ideas. They also help increase the visibility of the office of admissions among the faculty.

Summary

Student recruitment and admissions are important components of enrollment management and depend on the effectiveness of the office of admissions. Directors of admissions need to pay more attention to personnel management and office operations. Higher level administrators need to concern themselves more with the career concerns of their directors of admissions if they wish to avoid frequent turnover in that position. They also need to listen more carefully to the requests for increased staffing and funding. We have argued that even though financial stress is now reaching most colleges and universities, more resources may have to be devoted to student recruiting and admissions. However, there are also economical shortcuts to increased effectiveness. We have discussed several, including the use of adjunct recruiters and departmental liaison systems.

Having discussed ways to revitalize the office of admissions, we turn now to the most sensitive and controversial component of enrollment management—marketing in higher education.

CHAPTER 4
Linking Recruitment and Marketing

A good deal has been written about marketing and its uses in higher education. One would think from the number of advertised manuals and workshops that marketing offers the only real hope for institutional vitality. Unfortunately, marketing is not such a panacea. It can provide a more rational approach to student recruitment but only if one avoids the buzz words and gains a real understanding of marketing principles and their applicability to the unique environment of higher education. David Reisman puts the marketing issue in perspective:

> That a college adopts a marketing strategy is not necessarily a concession to crass commercialism for the sake of survival. It all depends on what the aims are and the means employed. At its best, college marketing can mean a careful survey of what distinctive segment of students a college is currently serving, whether it is adequately serving their needs as well as their wants, and whether there are enough such students likely to be available in the future so that the college can stay on course and maintain its traditional program. A marketing survey may discover that much recruiting effort is wasted; recruiters are sent to cities that are most unlikely to send students to the particular institution, while other areas that remain untouched have grown more affluent and better-educated, to give one kind of example, and might now provide a constituency if, through high school visits and in other ways, potential students and their families could be made aware of the institution and what it offers specifically for individuals of this sort and level. (Reisman, 1980, p. 105).

This chapter explores the concept of marketing. We show how marketing principles can be used to improve the effectiveness of institutional recruiting. The chapter includes an appraisal of the role outside marketing agencies can play in assisting institutions with enrollment management.

The Concept of Marketing

Marketing, in its simplest sense, means getting a useful product to the consumer. Noted marketing authority Philip Kotler offers this technical definition: "Marketing is the analysis, planning, implementation, and control of carefully formulated programs designed to bring about voluntary exchanges of values with target markets for the purpose of achieving organizational objectives. It relies heavily on designing the organization's offering in terms of the target markets' needs and desires, and on using effective pricing, communication, and distribution to inform, motivate, and serve markets" (Kotler, 1975, p. 5). Marketing literature first appeared in the early twentieth century. The concern initially was with the products, later with sales. More recently, businesses have taken a consumer orientation, seeking to identify consumer needs and then striving to meet them through product development and distribution.

Confusion about the Marketing Approach

Most administrators in higher education are confused about the marketing process. One survey of admissions directors at 350 private colleges and universities showed that nearly 90 percent of the respondents equated marketing with selling (Murphy and McGarrity, 1978). Fewer than three percent saw marketing as a combination of distinct strategies, such as planning, research, and product/program development. Although institutions often report they are doing "marketing," the majority have not undertaken many of the general tasks associated with marketing efforts. Blackburn (1980) identified sixteen specific techniques associated with marketing, ranging from current demand analysis to posttesting, then surveyed 720 admissions officers to assess their use of these techniques. He found the results contradictory, questioning "how the respondents were able to differentiate, position, and develop their institutions in the absence of market research" (p. 20). He also noted only 46 percent of the respondents had developed a specific marketing plan, even though such a plan is considered a prerequisite to successful marketing. According to a recent study by AACRAO and the College Board, nearly 50 percent of the 1,463 institutions surveyed did not conduct marketing studies and another 39 percent indicated they do so only informally (*Undergraduate Admissions,* 1980).

Necessity of Adaptation

Is it necessary that industrial-type marketing be incorporated wholesale into educational management? We think there are good reasons why the answer should be no. The characteristics of higher education and its governance process are sufficiently different from those of the industrial sector to warrant selective adaptation—not wholesale incorporation—of the marketing concept.

First, program development in higher education is largely a decentralized departmental function. It is not akin to highly centralized industrial product development. Thus, whereas program development is central to effective enrollment management, we do not classify it as a marketing task, though it would be one in the corporate sector.

Second, colleges and universities take a more active rather than passive stance toward markets. We are uncomfortable with the corporate notion that successful marketing involves going into the marketplace to ascertain consumer needs, then designing products and services to meet those needs. Institutions have philosophical goals that preclude changing their offerings to satisfy the ever-shifting demands of the marketplace. Veysey observes that "the key question concerns what actual compromises one is willing to make, either for survival or for maintenance of a student body at a given size" (Veysey, 1980, p. 28). Colleges and universities are educational institutions that also have social obligations. Greater awareness of these obligations in recent years has prompted many institutions to move away from electives to a more prescribed curricula. Colleges have to seek the proper balance between riding the waves of student interests and asserting that the institution exists to serve broader social needs.

Third, and perhaps most significantly, marketing has a negative image among academicians. To many, "marketing" is synonymous with promotional advertising at its worst. Rather than have the matter of effective enrollment management founder on the rocks of semantics, we chose to confine marketing within the context of student recruitment.

The components of marketing most useful to educational institutions include *research,* a *marketing plan, pricing, communication* with the external world, and an *assessment* program of recruitment activities. Each is discussed below, beginning with a background discussion of what kinds of recruiting methods are now being used.

As we have construed it, the concept of marketing can help administrators develop a coordinated and coherent recruitment program, which accurately portrays what the institution has to offer. Such a program will not only be reinforced by what enrolled students actually experience but will also help clarify the image of the institution to the general public. The result should be a closer match between institutional offerings and the expectations of potential students, resulting in higher yields of admitted applicants and lower attrition rates for enrolled students. Effective marketing should make selling unnecessary.

Understanding Current Recruitment Practices

Survey Results

In the 1981 National Enrollment Survey, we asked admissions directors to identify activities that have been expanded in recent years. The results of the survey appear in Table 7. New or "revitalized" promotional literature heads the list. The use of national mailing lists also ranks high. Increasingly, the literature on recruitment stresses the importance of effective advertising through promotional literature targeted to specific groups. (We will examine the merits of this strategy later in the chapter.) The high ratings given "travel" in Table 7 suggests that institutions are placing more emphasis on face-to-face external recruiting. Some studies suggest this emphasis may be misplaced because students indicate that college representatives have little influence on their matriculation decisions. Annual American Council on Education (ACE)/UCLA freshman survey data reveal that just 5 percent of entering 1981 freshmen indicated that college representatives

Table 7: Changes in Student Recruitment Program, 1975-1980
(percentage of admissions directors reporting increases)

Recruitment Activity	Public Research Univ.	AASCU Inst.	Public 2-Year Coll.	Private Univ.	Private 4-Year Coll.	Private 2-Year Coll.	All Inst.
New Promotion Literature	63	57	48	64	66	60	54
Travel	25	47	35	57	32	50	37
Recruit Adult Students	31	45	48	14	30	20	37
Special Market Research	25	27	20	50	51	40	35
Academic Dept. Recruitment	44	37	23	14	38	50	33
National Mailing Lists	47	34	16	36	43	30	31
Contact Special Groups (church, youth)	25	24	20	17	38	40	29
Recruit Part-Time Students	25	34	29	8	21	30	26
Recruit Ethnic Minorities	81	41	15	36	23	20	24
Use of Alumni	40	22	4	71	36	20	22
Attendance at Workshops	13	21	16	23	27	20	21
No Need Financial Aid	20	19	12	15	17	30	17
Cooperative Recruitment Programs	13	17	11	14	20	20	16
Special Admissions Task Force	31	28	7	15	19	10	15
Recruit Handicapped	13	13	20	15	1	0	11
Outside Consultants	0	5	7	17	11	20	10
Recruit Foreign Students	0	10	4	29	13	10	9
Recruit Veterans	13	14	10	0	4	0	7
Recruit U.S. Students from Abroad	0	2	0	21	8	10	5

influenced their decision to attend a particular college. Only teachers had less influence on enrollment decisions (4 percent).

Heading the list were the academic reputation of the institution (51 percent), followed by education programs (27 percent) (Astin, King, and Richardson, 1982). Of course, these data do not acknowledge the role the recruiter plays in promoting awareness of the institution and its programs. Similarly, car buyers cite the quality of the car and not their relationship with the salesperson as the reason for selecting a particular model. So it is among personnel and potential students. The catalytic role of the go-between is overlooked. Posters, literature about the institution, personal contact with interested students, and the school counselor—all serve an important marketing function.

Major Recruitment Trends

Table 7 shows that institutions have also expanded or upgraded a variety of other recruiting practices in recent years.

Alumni Involvement. Admissions directors at 71 percent of the private universities and 36 percent of private four-year colleges are currently increasing this dimension of recruiting. Thirty-five percent of the admissions directors plan to increase this area in the future; for public universities and AASCU institutions the percentages are comparatively low—27 percent and 33 percent, respectively. Many institutions, especially those that are former teacher training colleges, overlook the role their alumni serving in high schools and community colleges can play in recruiting.

Recruitment of nontraditional students. Admissions personnel have not reduced efforts to recruit nontraditional students, such as minorities and the handicapped. The biggest new push for minority recruitment is the public sector, mainly in universities. Although 13 percent of admissions directors in public colleges and universities say they are increasing the recruitment of handicapped students, few at private colleges say they are doing so.

Recruitment of adults. Public institutions are the front-runners in the area of adult recruitment. Most private institutions are more likely to cater by desire or necessity to full-time students, with less attention to most adult learners. Most of the admissions directors who say they plan to increase recruiting of adults are in the public sector, though 40 percent of directors at private two-year colleges say they plan to do so. (Data not shown.)

Despite the long list of possible recruiting activities, however, most institutions seem to place most of their efforts on two or three traditional approaches. Data collected by AACRAO and the College Board in 1979 show the top three recruitment tools to be high school visitation (78 percent), direct mail (64 percent), and attendance at college nights/fairs (64 percent). The least reported methods involve traditional "marketing" on radio or television, in high school newspapers, on billboards and buses or subways, and in professional journals (all less than 10 percent) (*Undergraduate Admissions,* 1980). It is doubtful that most institutions systematically assess recruitment techniques to determine their effectiveness. Now let us explore marketing techniques useful to education.

Setting Up An Enrollment Research System

Most colleges and universities do not have a systematic research program related to enrollment management. Two types of research are essential to providing an effective enrollment information system—market studies and institutional research. Some commentators lump the two together. We have chosen to separate enrollment research into two categories, one focusing primarily on the character of the external environment and the other directed at the institution and its constituencies.

Market Studies and Institutional Research

Market studies provide information about such matters as demographic changes, future employment needs, sources of potential student pools, and the enrollment trends of competing colleges and universities. Market studies are essential to determine future enrollment, yet only slightly more than half the colleges and universities in the country even conduct enrollment projections (*Undergraduate Admissions,* 1980).

Institutional research focuses on two types of data: baseline statistical data and student attitudinal data. Baseline statistical information charts the flow of students from application through graduation. These data include size of the applicant pool, number and percentage admitted, and number and percentage of freshmen, transfers, and graduate students enrolled. Various descriptors, such as sex, race, location, high school rank, and intended major, provide additional valuable information. For example, if the data show that a majority of applicants live within 50 miles of the institution and the second largest group comes from beyond 100 miles, it may be to the institution's advantage to focus more recruiting efforts on students in the 50-100 mile range.

Data can also be obtained on "stalled" students and student dropouts, as well as on shifts in student academic majors. Some institutions have developed early warning systems, which spot potential dropouts among their entering students by using information provided by the office of institutional research, institutional breakouts from such national surveys as UCLA's Cooperative Institutional Research Program (CIRP), and information provided by the national testing agencies.

Student attitudinal information reveals what influences students' application, matriculation, and attrition behavior. Attitudinal information also provides a means of assessing the impact of institutional recruiting efforts; examples of the types of surveys yielding such information are listed in Table 8.

Survey instruments for some of the categories in Table 8 are available from such organizations as UCLA's Cooperative Institutional Research Program, the Educational Testing Service (ETS), the National Center for Higher Education Management Systems (NCHEMS), and the College Board. Many colleges have developed their own survey instruments and administer them periodically to acquire longitudinal data. However, one important advantage of a nationally used instrument is the availability of institutional norms. Additionally, they often cost less, yet provide more data. Where time and money are pressing concerns, telephone surveys can provide data quickly and cheaply.

An Example: North Texas State University

North Texas State University, wanted to assess its image in state high schools and community colleges. A telephone survey to a carefully drawn sample of high school and community college counselors was developed. With a 70 percent response rate, the

Table 8: Components of Attitudinal Institutional Research

Survey of Freshmen, Transfer, Graduate Applicants to Determine What Factors Prompted Them to Apply

- Directory information (sex, age, high school grades, high school rank, etc.)
- Reasons for applying
- Comparison with competitors

Survey of Admitted Students Who Did Not Enroll

- Directory information
- Reasons for not enrolling

Survey of Newly Enrolled Students

- Directory information
- Reasons for enrolling

Survey of High School and Transfer Counselors

- Image of institution
- Evaluation of recruiting compared with competition
- Evaluation of information about campus and programs

Survey of Dropouts

- Directory information
- What doing now?
- Factors causing dropout
- Attitude toward campus service

Survey of Enrolled Students

- Directory information
- Attitude toward campus service

Survey of Graduates

- Directory information
- What doing now?
- Reactions to college
- Suggestions for change

survey rapidly provided extremely valuable information about the university's image and recruiting practices.

The telephone survey revealed that the university's image varied significantly among individual high school and community college counselors. From one perspective, this ambiguous image could be viewed as an impediment to the university's recruitment program: an unclear image could be synonymous with a negative image. Roger Campbell speaks of the institutional myths an incoherent communication system can create.

> *Institutional mythology is a byproduct of incoherency or of institutional signals that lack coherence. You must assume that, if your messages have not been clear, or if they are mixed in any way, the recipient will be forced to unscramble them. This unscrambling process creates institutional myths. You describe yourself in part, other segments of your campus flash a different type of message, and the recipient must unscrample what they have heard and arrive at some conclusion. These conclusions become institutional myths (Campbell, 1981, p. 14).*

The danger of myths is that students will be attracted to the institution for the wrong reasons. Some will quickly become disenchanted and drop out. The task of the campus is to conduct the necessary research to uncover institutional myths and the practices that perpetuate them.

The North Texas State University telephone survey results, coupled with other data, led the institution to confront the issue of its public image. Furthermore, the data also raised the question of image consistency. Do internal constituencies hold the same image of the institution as does the public? Another important byproduct was better information about recruitment practices. The admissions task force was surprised to learn that counselors were dissatisfied with the kind and quantity of literature available about North Texas State, including the university's catalog. Although it takes time to develop new and improved recruitment literature, there was no need for the university to delay sending counselors additional copies of current materials. Thus, survey results contributed to solving short- and long-term problems:

the counselors' need for literature and the university's need to clarify its image.

In addition to surveys, in-depth interviews are a rich source of information unobtainable in other ways. Many institutions already do this through exit interviews for students who withdraw at mid-term. Conducting interviews with prospective students who don't enroll and with recent graduates could also be profitable.

Use of Data in Enrollment Planning

One way or another, acquiring trend and attitudinal information, in combination with information about changes in the external market, helps campus officials make more tutored decisions affecting academic, recruitment, and retention programs. Once obtained, the information should have a simple format and be widely disseminated to administrators and faculty members. Probably the greatest barrier to using such research in campus decision-making is the tendency for administrators to present data in an incomprehensible manner (see Baldridge and Tierney, 1979). To illustrate how complex data can be simplified by summation in tabular fashion, we have included in Appendix A several reporting forms for trend data on student recruitment.

The directors of admissions we interviewed fully understood the importance of an enrollment information system. Most saw it as a way to advance their views to administrators and faculty. However, many have difficulty obtaining such information because institutional research is often conducted by a different office, which responds to a different set of priorities. The increasing use of microcomputers may offer a partial solution to this problem, since they provide access to data and allow operators to do enrollment forecasting and simulation.

With microcomputers, users have full access to their own data base, which they develop. Because an admissions office with on-line data access via micro, mini, or main-frame computers is not dependent upon other offices for either data-gathering or analysis, it has control over its research needs. Moreover, the comparatively low cost of microcomputers may be an attractive alternative, especially for small colleges, to costly processing through centralized units. The availability of low-cost word processing programs from commercial sources enhances the utility of microcomputers in offices with little or no computing resources.

Developing a Marketing Plan

The second component of the marketing concept for higher education is a marketing plan. A marketing plan cannot be formulated until the mission and goals of the institution are determined. An enrollment information system (as described in the previous section) can provide useful information to a committee charged with clarifying the campus' mission and goals. The aim of such a group should be to arrive at a clear statement describing the college, focusing on its uniquenesses. The research can help anchor the mission statement in reality. Overblown statements, which only serve to perpetuate institutional myths, should be avoided. Grabowski (1981) cites the tendency for college mission statements to be modeled after each other, noting that one of his students came across the same paragraph in the bulletins of two different schools complete with the same typographical error!

Since faculty play such an important role in enrollment management, it is essential that the substance of the proposed mission statement be shared with the entire campus community, and an opportunity be provided to debate the recommendations of the committee. Finally, the spirit of the final document should be expressed in a manner having the broadest possible appeal.

Once an enrollment information system has been set up and the institution's mission clarified, a marketing plan can be developed, complete with goals and timetables. A marketing plan can be relatively brief, stating specific recruiting goals and a timetable, or it can be elaborate, detailing implementation strategies and responsibilities. Carnegie-Mellon University, for example, has a 143-page plan that outlines in considerable detail its strategies for finding and recruiting prospective students.

Marketing plans usually spell out primary and secondary markets. The *primary market* is a high yield market: a large proportion of the applicants attend the college upon admission. For all but the most selective colleges, the primary market is the region immediately surrounding the institution, since students tend to select colleges fairly close to home. Increasing costs are likely to reinforce this tendency in the future. Once a primary market has been identified, the admissions staff should protect and nurture it. An additional investment in time and money in the primary market will usually bring about a greater return of matriculants than a similar investment elsewhere.

Beyond a certain radius, the college will find its *secondary market,* which is basically a low yield market. A college may receive a steady flow of applicants from this market, but few of these students will actually enroll because often the college is the student's second or third choice. More focused recruiting might increase the number of applications from a secondary market, but first the campus should clarify and sharpen its image in this region. Doing so will help eliminate inaccuracies about the campus, which may account in part for the relatively small number of applications and low applicant yield.

Some commentators suggest that, resources permitting, institutions should consider establishing a third or "test-market." Considerable time and money will be necessary to cultivate this third market, but increases in applications and admissions may offset decreases triggered by demographic or economic changes in the primary and secondary markets.

Positioning and Segmentation in a Market

Positioning an institution in a particular market simply means identifying the characteristics of the institution and contrasting them with competing institutions. The goal is to differentiate the institution from its competitors. If enrollment research has been carefully conducted and an accurate mission statement developed, positioning should be relatively easy.

Segmentation refers to identifying different types of students who might be attracted to the institution and developing special recruitment literature and practices for them. For example, market studies led SUNY-Geneseo to conclude that considerable numbers of qualified community college transfer students could be attracted to the college. Consequently, the college developed articulation agreements between academic departments and two-year institutions in western New York. One admissions staff member was assigned the title of transfer admissions counselor and scheduled to recruit solely from local community colleges. A brochure for transfer students was developed, as was a special newsletter for community college counselors to keep them up to date on changes in transfer policies and provide other campus news. A survey of recently enrolled transfer students was undertaken, and based on its results, special services were arranged to meet transfer student needs. Such efforts resulted in an increase in the number of applications from community college students.

An Example: Old Dominion University

One of our case study institutions, Old Dominion University (ODU) in Norfolk, Virginia, spent a good part of the 1970s defining its mission, locating its primary recruiting area, and revitalizing its office of admissions. Old Dominion University, a former branch campus of the College of William and Mary that became a full-fledged university in 1969, operated without a recruiting strategy in 1971. Of twelve publicly funded universities, Old Dominion ranked last in state appropriations. Beginning that year, the university made a concerted effort to establish its identity as a multipurpose university. One of the first tasks was to clarify its mission as an urban institution. As eventually developed, its mission statement consists of seven programmatic themes: administration, applied science and technology, development of urban educators, fine and performing arts, health-related studies, international studies, and marine and environmental studies. Since most of its students come from the Tidewater area in and around Norfolk, the university makes special effort to localize its message. Such factors as regional pride, convenience, and cost are highlighted in publications geared to this primary recruiting market. As its primary market, the Tidewater area continues to receive the largest share of ODU's recruiting effort. Admissions personnel visit area high schools three or four times a year and conduct special activities for counselors once a year on the ODU campus; they encourage students who are admitted to enroll through a systematic reinforcement program. Off-campus centers have kept the university abreast of population shifts in and around the Tidewater area.

At the same time, ODU has expanded its marketing program into its secondary market beyond the Tidewater region. They have made a special effort to promote the urban image of the campus in northern Virginia and the northeast urban corridor including New Jersey, downstate New York, and western Connecticut. Using alumni in these areas has helped to improve ODU's application-to-enrollment yield.

Old Dominion University's Enrollment Services Division has helped graduate departments at the university increase enrollments by advising them to develop special course packages within existing degree programs. For example, a military history concentration has been developed for persons stationed at the 72 military installations in the Norfolk area.

Determining an Effective Pricing System

In the past several years, interest has grown in using financial aid as an inducement to enrollment. The AACRAO and College Board survey reveals that about half the surveyed colleges offer no-need scholarships and about one-third use modified aid packages. This money is used primarily to attract academically qualified or specially talented students to the campus (*Undergraduate Admissions*, 1980). Cost has become an important factor in college selection, in large part because of rapidly rising tuition and living costs and the decline in available federal aid. Until recently, few institutions were concerned with using variable pricing as a recruiting tool. Today there is increasing interest in determining how cost affects student choice, particularly at private institutions which have greater pricing flexibility than those in the public sector.

Grabowski (1981) has identified several pricing models relevant to higher education. They include (1) *stratified pricing,* where tuition is based on the actual costs of a student's major; (2) *scaled pricing,* where the tuition students pay decreases with the number of courses taken up to a normal load and increases thereafter; (3) *two-part pricing,* which separates the cost of fixed overhead from the actual cost of each course; (4) *semester pricing,* where students pay a flat fee for each semester regardless of the number of courses taken; (5) *unit pricing,* where prices vary depending on whether the student is full-time or part-time and on when and where the course is taken, for example, at night and on weekends.

Since the development of an effective pricing system is quite complex, we cannot cover it here in depth. Interested readers are advised to consult the literature in this area, especially Huddleston and Batty (1978), Ihlanfeldt (1980), and Spence and Weathersby (1981).

Improving Communication with Prospective Students

As Table 7 indicates, most campuses are now busy developing recruitment literature. The danger, of course, is that the literature may inflate expectations about campus resources. Everyone loses when the student arrives on campus to discover that the music program that seemed impressive in the catalog consists of only two faculty members supplemented by a paltry performance program. Considering the money and time expended on developing new promotional literature, it makes little sense to enroll more students if the result is an increase in student attrition. Such puffery also threatens to undermine relations with competing institutions. Fortunately, results from the National Enrollment Survey show that unethical recruiting practices are not yet widespread. Only 15 percent of the directors of admissions responding feel that this issue has been a problem for them.

Prepublication Assessment

Before new publications are developed, considerable research should be done. Examining existing publications will determine what needs to be revised or even deleted. Are existing publications accurate? Do they reach their intended audiences? Are they viewed favorably? Do they duplicate other materials? Are they effective? Similar questions should be raised about new publications. One recent study of a nationwide sample of college recruitment literature shows the reading level to be appropriate for advanced college students. Many of the terms used, especially in catalogs, were frequently beyond the comprehension of the recent high school graduate. (Johnson and Chapman, 1979).

An equally valid question is whether the new publication is needed at all. Research by Litton (1981) suggests that some messages may best be conveyed by other means. Litton, in association with the College Board, surveyed 2,000 parents of high-school seniors with high Preliminary Scholastic Aptitude Test (PSAT) scores to assess the types of information they desire about colleges and the preferred source for this information. The results of the survey, which was conducted in six metropolitan regions of the country, appear in Table 9.

The respondents identified seven items as the most important thing to know about a college. Financial aid heads the list. Interestingly, "general academic reputation" rated sixth.

Note that in Table 9 alumni and enrolled students are viewed as effective sources for some types of information. If marshalled effectively, recent alumni and enrolled students can be very convincing recruiters. Unfortunately, most institutions have not tapped these sources. Even where students and alumni are used to communicate with prospective students, they often do not know enough about specific college programs and policies to be helpful. Indeed, even admissions personnel frequently are not knowledgeable about college programs and services. Given the reliance of the parents surveyed in the Litton study on admissions counselors for financial and academic program information, such ignorance can be costly.

College publications were the preferred source for only one type of information—fields of study. Of course, college publications can incorporate some of the other sources through presentation of testimonials, survey data, and the like. But simply doing so ought not to lead one to conclude that an institution's publications are now important inducements to enrollment. Only field testing can confirm that fact.

Maximizing the Impact of Direct Mail

Recent research shows that not only do admissions officers expect to increase their direct mail of printed materials but that they also believe catalogs and informational brochures are effective recruiting tools (Chapman, 1981). Yet students place less emphasis on printed matter than on the views of their parents, cost, where their friends choose to go to school, and availability of programs. Based on his research, Chapman concludes that students "read the printed materials primarily to confirm decisions they have made already on other grounds" (p. 501).

Most admissions directors are familiar with direct mail, and some are quite proficient at using it. The University of Pittsburgh recently won top prize from the Direct Mail Market Association for its direct mail efforts. In most cases, admissions personnel obtain mailing lists of students with certain desirable charac-

Table 9: Preferred Types and Sources of Information About College
(percentages of parents responding)

Preferred Types of Infor.*	Preferred Sources								
	High School Coun.	College Admis. Coun.	Coll. Fac.	College Alumni	Current Students	Parents Enrolled Students	Coll. Pubs	Com-merical Pubs	Other
Financial Aid	7	**48**	2	1	4	5	29	4	–
Fields of Study	17	23	11	4	3	–	**37**	3	2
Faculty Teaching Reputation	16	6	13	**27**	17	–	3	10	8
Academic Standards	17	10	**21**	15	6	1	9	11	10
Careers	15	20	13	**26**	4	–	12	4	6
General Academic Reputation	**23**	6	3	16	7	3	10	16	16
Social Atmosphere	3	4	3	14	**60**	5	5	2	4

*Listed in order of preference

Boldface indicates highest percentages.

Source: Litton, 1981.

teristics from the testing agencies, scholarship programs, commercial vendors, or state and local agencies. The problem is that large numbers of colleges and universities do the very same thing. Nearly 70 percent of the institutions using direct mail target their efforts to the academically talented student (*Undergraduate Admissions*, 1980). As a result, prospective students in the top quarter of their high school classes are deluged with mail—as many as several hundred pieces in some cases.

In light of the questionable effectiveness of printed material as a recruiting tool, colleges should question the wisdom of using such services, especially if the college or university does not normally attract a high calibre student. For example, colleges that attempt to attract students with a Scholastic Aptitude Test (SAT)-Verbal score of 550 or better from families with incomes in excess of $20,000 annually limit themselves to less than 10 percent of all high school graduates. Bright students deluged with fancy posters, flyers, and "personalized" word-processed letters will quickly eliminate most of the senders, if only because they appear to be trying too hard.

Some campuses have applied a more discriminating approach to direct mail. For example, SUNY College at Potsdam's Marketing Task Force recommended that the college use direct mail to contact alumni with college-age children, alumni employed in public schools and community colleges, and parents of enrolled students. Tastefully done, such direct mail efforts are likely to be more effective than blanket mailings to thousands of students, most of whom have no knowledge of the institution.

Assessing Recruitment Activities

When confronted with an enrollment problem, some high-level administrators employ the "throw money" strategy: to solve a problem, throw money at it. Ihlanfeldt notes that it is not unusual for campuses to spend more than $1,000 to enroll one student (1980, p. 1). Recruiting is expensive, and in these cost-conscious times it makes sense to be sure the institution is spending its money wisely.

Assessment is essential, and it should be conducted for each recruitment-related activity. Assessment *criteria* include cost, number of applicants and enrollees generated, time, staffing requirements, and attitude. Attitude is included because the impact of an activity on the attitude of a prospective student about the campus may be very important for some types of assessments. Some of our case study institutions solicit the reactions of prospective, admitted, and enrolled students to various recruitment and admissions practices. For example, students are asked to evaluate their campus interview session, campus tour guides, the quality of campus publications, the new student orientation session, and so on.

Assessment *techniques* include surveys, financial audits, statistical compilations, and interviews. Obviously, it is important to match assessment techniques with assessment criteria. Thus, surveys will elicit attitudinal information but not statistical trend data.

Assessment should also include the activities of recruiters. Many campuses consider it standard operating procedure to keep a record for each recruiter of schools visited, number of students seen, number who eventually applied, number admitted, and number enrolled. A rating system can also be devised to assess the quality of the reception received at the visited school. (A sample chart for recording this information is contained in Appendix A.) The results of this assessment system will not only guide future recruiting efforts but also help determine the most appropriate sites for visits by individual college recruiters.

Of course, assessment can become burdensome, and too much will overwhelm the admissions office with additional paperwork, as well as undermine morale. An assessment program should be devised that itself will survive a cost/benefit analysis.

Using Outside Marketing Agencies

One alternative facing colleges with enrollment problems is to hire an outside marketing firm. We found that only 33 percent of college and university presidents in the National Enrollment Survey indicated they had used the services of such a firm. The percentages were highest for private four-year and two-year institutions (20 and 22 percent, respectively) and lowest for public universities (10 percent).

Those responding to this question in the affirmative were asked to indicate their degree of satisfaction with the firm's work. Six percent said they were not satisfied, 33 percent said they were uncertain, and 40 percent said the results were satisfactory in the short term. Another 18 percent said they were unsure how to evaluate the services provided. Only three percent said they were satisfied over both the short and long term.

These responses suggest that employing a marketing firm is not an automatic solution to enrollment problems. Institutions faced with severe enrollment shortfalls are understandably searching for answers and may find themselves easily persuaded of the benefits such firms proclaim. We urge those in this situation to be wary. There are some things a marketing firm can do well, but relying on an outside agency is no substitute for taking the effort to put one's own house in order.

This is not to say that outside marketing firms cannot provide some useful services. For one thing, an external agency can provide in-service training for admissions and other personnel who lack background in marketing, particularly if the external agency specializes in higher education or is sponsored by a higher education professional association. Marketing firms also have the necessary hardware to develop brochures, films, and other recruitment materials. Marketing firms can usually produce these materials quickly, avoiding costly delays and enabling campus officials to show that something is being done to meet an enrollment problem.

But there are disadvantages as well. One of the liabilities of relying on an external firm is that it tends to reinforce the faculty's view that enrollment management is someone else's job. Relying on a marketing firm fosters a dangerous dependence, which not only ignores institutional capabilities to do the same thing for less but also keeps the campus community from coming to grips with its own problems. For example, only the faculty and administration working together can effectively update and improve curriculum or develop programs to lower a skyrocketing attrition rate. In fact, the efforts of an external agency can be counterproductive if the recruiting program ultimately designed portrays the institution as something it is not, thus both deluding prospective students and angering members of the campus community.

External agencies also are not equipped to develop and maintain the kinds of sophisticated enrollment information systems discussed above. To be effective, such systems require recruitment and retention information particular to an institution's situation. In general, only campus personnel have sufficient insight to ask the right questions. Finally, an external marketing firm is expensive. Precious dollars are siphoned off from an institution already in financial difficulty. In sum, a marketing or public relations firm, if it is to be used at all, ought to be used to augment, not replace, the campus' efforts to solve its own enrollment problems.

Summary

Marketing is not a cure-all to current and future enrollment problems in higher education. But if selectively adapted to the characteristics of higher education, marketing can help institutions do a better job of student recruitment. First, market studies and institutional research need to be conducted, for the establishment and use of an enrollment information system is essential to the development of an accurate mission statement and to construction of a marketing plan.

Communication strategies should be developed and tested with regard to student recruitment. Offices of admissions must devote more effort to tailoring recruitment strategies to their own situations. Because the research demonstrates that there are no tried and true methods for recruiting students, reliance on school-by-school recruiting or direct mail may not be the most effective recruiting techniques for an individual campus.

In short, administrators concerned with enrollment management have every reason to be creative, to experiment, and to assess the effectiveness of the strategies they devise to recruit students. The goal in every case ought to be to let the institution sell itself. For this to occur, administrators and faculty need to work together to see that communication with potential students in any form accurately portrays what the campus has to offer. Marketing firms can help but cannot be regarded as a substitute for faculty and administrative efforts to seek creative solutions to their own enrollment problems.

CHAPTER 5
Improving Student Retention

An enormous number of students drop out before they finish college. This continuing problem sharply compounds the current shortfall in enrollments. Throughout the higher education community there is newly awakened interest in student attrition, but only in a few scattered cases, are vigorous efforts being mounted to deal with this critical problem.

From the outset it should be clear that all student attrition is not necessarily bad. Lenning, Beal, and Saver clarify the problem:

> *Some students need to transfer, stop out, or drop out for their own benefit, and an approach that could somehow force them to stay would be inappropriate, in spite of the detrimental financial implications of decreased enrollment. . . . Rather than improving retention per se, the primary goal should be to better meet student needs and to provide a more meaningful educational experience. And in the long run, motivations closer to the mission of the institution probably will lead to higher enrollments and tuition revenue than will a short-sighted, survivalist focus on enrollments for enrollments' sake (1980, p. 16).*

Despite all the concern about shrinking recruitment pools, college presidents whose institutions had enrollment problems

---

Note: Parts of this chapter are taken from Baldridge, Kemerer, and Green (1982). This source is briefly discussed in Appendix B. "Sources for Further Reading."

identified student attrition as the number one culprit (Stadtman, 1980, Table 39). In our National Enrollment Survey, an impressive 85 percent of college presidents agree that "[their] institution[s] should devote more attention and resources to the issue of student retention and reducing the dropout rate." The interest in increasing retention was uniformly high across all types of institutions.

The Dimensions of the Attrition Problem

Dropout rates vary substantially among institutions. Our survey of college admissions directors reveals that attrition rates for freshmen are highest at public community colleges and lowest at private universities (Figure 6). Public four-year colleges and universities also have high attrition rates. Overall, only 20 percent of the admissions directors report a freshman attrition rate of under 15 percent, 38 percent report freshman attrition rates of between 16 and 25 percent, and 42 percent lose over one-quarter of their freshman classes.

When asked to compare freshman and total undergraduate attrition rates of today with those of five years ago, over half of the admissions directors report little change. Thirty-five percent report less freshman attrition than five years ago, and only nine percent report more. The percentages are about the same for total undergraduate attrition. The five-year comparisons do not vary significantly by institutional type, although a larger proportion of admissions directors at public four-year colleges report increased attrition among freshmen and undergraduates (14 and 15 percent, respectively).

Our research, together with the findings of others, demonstrates that:

• Roughly half the students who enter a four-year institution never graduate from that institution. Among the half that leave the institution, however, a substantial number transfer to other colleges and eventually finish. Roughly 30 percent of the entering freshmen in four-year colleges never receive a bachelor's degree.

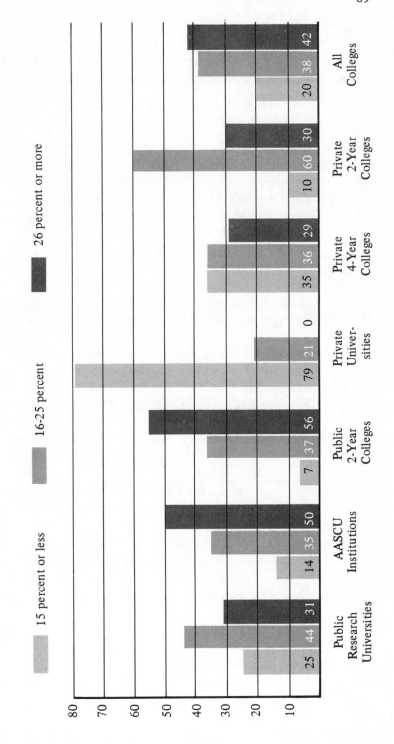

Figure 6. Freshman Attrition Rate by Institutional Type in 1981
(*percentages as reported by admissions directors*)

- Community colleges have a much higher dropout rate than have four-year institutions. Approximately 60 percent of community college freshmen never complete an associate degree program, and over 80 percent never complete a bachelor's degree program.

- Private four-year institutions have slightly higher five-year graduation rates (60 percent) than public four-year institutions (roughly 53 percent).

- The more prestigious an institution, the lower its attrition rate. Very selective institutions have low dropout rates; at the other extreme, "open-admission" unselective community colleges have extremely high dropout rates.

- Institutions with large commuter enrollments have high dropout rates, and institutions with strong residential dormitory programs have lower than average dropout rates.

Not only do different types of institutions have different dropout rates, but the student's chances of dropping out are also substantially different. Men drop out more frequently than women, minorities drop out more than whites, low-ability students drop out at much higher rates than high-ability students, and low-income students drop out more than high-income students.

Students who are socially integrated into a campus are much more likely to receive a degree than those who are socially isolated (Astin, 1975). Socially integrated students are more likely to live in a dormitory, have a part-time job on the campus, participate in clubs and fraternities, and declare an academic major early in their college career. Persisters are enmeshed in the social web of the campus: they have a high degree of social interaction with their fellow students and with faculty and are deeply involved in academic and social life.

By contrast, the socially isolated student is more likely to be a commuter, to live off-campus, to be undeclared about an academic program, to have little interaction with student peers and faculty, and to have very high vocational orientation. Astin argues that colleges could have substantial impact on attrition rates by dealing with the social integration issue.

As already stated, freshmen have substantially higher dropout rates than any other group. The attrition problem in many respects is basically a freshman problem. Of the 50 percent who typically leave a four-year institution, fully three out of five leave during their freshman year. Or to put it another way, if a college has an attrition problem, roughly 60 percent of the loss occurs among freshmen. This has important implications for administrative action. To cut the attrition rate, the college should concentrate much of its efforts on freshmen.

Unfortunately, many institutions do not have accurate retention data. Recognizing that accurate data are essential for any retention efforts, the Southern California Retention Consortium developed two forms to help monitor attrition rates. (Both are included as Forms IV and V in Appendix A.) One form focuses on *annual attrition* while the other addresses *cohort attrition*.

Annual attrition refers to the number of students who drop out of the college each year. Annual attrition monitors the annual flow of students into, through, and out of the college: how many start, how many graduate, and how many drop out during the course of the year. Careful monitoring of these numbers can help signal major enrollment problems. For example, what if the annual attrition rate had been stable for several years and then increased suddenly? This might suggest some significant changes in environmental forces (such as government aid for college students) or in college programs (new grading standards or deteriorating campus services) that affect attrition. Longitudinal data on the annual attrition rate help identify shifts that could have a severe impact on enrollments and revenues.

Cohort attrition data help track retention and graduation rates of entering freshmen classes. These are generally the figures institutions cite when discussing retention and attrition: the percentage of entering freshmen who returned for the sophomore year and then went on to earn degrees. As these data have been widely reported for different types of institutions, it is relatively easy to compare individual retention rates against the norm for similar types of colleges and universities (public four-year colleges, private universities, etc.). Cohort data help institutions track the impact of program innovations on groups of students. For example, has the new freshman advising program helped improve retention? A quick check of the freshman retention rate for the past several classes might reveal a marked improvement. Consequently, cohort data are also important to institutional efforts to monitor and cut attrition.

The Financial Costs of Attrition

How much does it cost the institution in dollars when a student drops out? Regardless of institutional type, college finances are heavily dependent on student enrollments. At first glance, it may seem that private colleges are more dependent on student-driven financial resources than are their public counterparts. In fact, 70 percent or more of the total revenue of a typical private college is generated by direct student tuition payments. The other 30 percent is usually indirectly related to enrollments—dorm fees, bookstore revenues, and food service finances. Only a small part of a private college's revenue—funds from endowments and gifts—are unrelated to current student enrollments.

What about public institutions? Almost every formula for state funding depends primarily on a student count of some kind. A subsidy is usually awarded to an institution by counting its full-time equivalent (FTE) enrollment figures on a designated census date. Consequently, public four-year institutions are highly sensitive to enrollment fluctuations, just as private institutions are.

Public community colleges are also highly enrollment sensitive. Many are in the same situation as public four-year institutions—funding based on FTE enrollments, as determined by class counts. Other public community colleges, those in California, for example, are even more attuned to enrollment fluctuations because their funding is calculated from average daily attendance (ADA) formulas. Instead of counting the enrollment on a census date once a semester, these institutions count enrollments every single day, a hold-over from the time when community colleges were extensions of public school systems. Public institutions that use ADA formulas literally have their pulses checked daily and their finances adjusted accordingly.

In short, the funding of almost every type of higher education institution is based squarely on its enrollment. Whether the
money comes directly from tuition payments or indirectly from
state subsidies, the fact remains—students bring the money. When
enrollments drop, revenue is lost, and it is this fact that is causing
the concern over the financial impact of attrition.

Students enter college with different financial resources.
Most private colleges estimate that their students contribute
approximately $2,000 per year out of their own pockets. Stu-
dents also receive directly a variety of federal and state grants
or loans. When a student drops out, this money, which would
have paid for part of the student's tuition, also leaves the institution.

Of course the impact of student attrition on finances is
rather different for private colleges and universities than it is for
public institutions. In private colleges and universities, the impact
is fairly immediate through the loss of tuition income. In public
institutions, the loss of income by student attrition depends on
the individual state's financial policies for higher education. For
this reason it is important to examine the private and public
sectors separately.

Financial Costs at Private Institutions

When a student drops out of a private college or university,
the impact is felt immediately through the loss of tuition. It is
important, however, to examine the *mix* of funds that a student
brings to the campus in order to pay tuition. Generally the campus
does not lose all of the tuition because, in reality, the student
brought only part of the funds; the remainder was provided by
institutional scholarships and outside aid.

This can be explained by the fact that a student's tuition is
composed of four parts: the student's contribution, the student's
financial aid received directly from federal or state agencies,
institutionally awarded grants or loans and work-study payments,
and a tuition discount. When a student drops out, the instituion
loses the first two sources of funds. Institutionally awarded
financial aid can be saved and reallocated to another student,
whereas the tuition discount is more like an investment the college makes in its students. The institution does not actually

award dollars; it merely discounts the tuition by a certain percentage.

Let's look at a concrete example of how attrition financially hurts an institution through tuition losses.

Acme College, a fictional institution similar to one of the consortium colleges where we conducted interviews for this study, charges $3,600 in tuition and fees. If Acme sets an enrollment goal of 700 students and falls short by 50 students, Acme will lose $137,900 and not $180,000. How was this number derived?

As mentioned earlier, the institution will lose only two out of the four tuition resources: the student's contribution, which is $2,178, and whatever outside federal or state financial aid the student received (estimated to equal $580 per student). Thus, the institution loses only $2,758 per student rather than all $3,600 of the tuition. Hence, a drop of 50 students equals a revenue loss of $137,900 ($2,758 X 50).

What if Acme College had been able to retain an extra 50 students? Rather than an enrollment of 700, Acme College now has 750 students. The college will obviously increase its tuition revenue by $180,000 but it will have to subtract from this amount the higher tuition discount it will give to the additional 50 students. Let us suppose that Acme College gives each extra student an additional $500 discount because the college's work-study and other federal funds have already been allocated to other students. This $25,000 ($500 X 50) will then be subtracted from the $180,000 tuition surplus, netting a surplus revenue of $155,000.

Therefore, when students drop out of a private college or university, the college does lose a significant portion of the tuition and fees that the students bring with them; however, the institution is also able to recoup a portion of the lost revenue because of the financial aid mix each student receives.

Financial Costs at Public Institutions

When a student leaves a public college or university, the institution loses funds, but the magnitude of that loss depends in large measure on state funding policies. In the past, it was common practice to have a direct linkage between a student subsidy and the student. That is, the state provided a fixed number of dollars for every student enrolled in the institution. If the state provided $4,000 per student and 50 students dropped out, the institution would almost surely lose $200,000. Of course, the *timing* of the attrition is important. A student who dropped out in the middle of the year might not have the funds withdrawn by the state. But undoubtedly that drop out would lead to diminished funds in the next year.

When the funding is based on a direct-linkage formula, the financial impact of attrition is immediate and direct. Since all the funds basically come from one source, the state's formula can cause the loss of almost all of the subsidy for a drop out. In fact, in this situation student attrition actually hurts public institutions more than private institutions because the *mix* of funds is not available for reallocation. By contrast, private institutions make up their tuition from a variety of contributions, including family payments, outside aid, and internal scholarships. This mix allows more reallocation of funds in private institutions than is possible in public institutions.

In recent years, however, this lockstep relationship between funds and students has been broken in many state formulas. More and more states are attempting to make more sophisticated *incremental* analyses of costs. In an institution with 15,000 students the addition of 100 more students simply does not cost proportionally more. There are economies of scale, and additional students at the margin cost less in most situations. The reverse is also true: to drop 100 students in a 20,000 student institution simply does not save the institution very much money. This more sophisticated incremental analysis has led to funding changes. In general, many large public institutions now operate under formulas where only a portion of an increase or a decrease is awarded or penalized.

For example, Western State University—another fictional institution—has a budget base of 15,000 FTE students and receives a subsidy of $4,000 per student. Now, if Western State University increases the size of its student body by 100 students, the state's formula provides that the incremental subsidy will be only $1,800 per student; likewise the state will take away only $1,800 per student for a shortfall below the base budget.

The first impression, then, is that a larger number of dropouts does not really hurt the institution because it only has to pay back a portion of the loss under an incremental budgeting formula. That conclusion is very deceptive because it ignores what happens the *next* year. If the state is sophisticated enough to have an incremental budgeting system, it is also sophisticated enough to monitor enrollments very carefully. The likely outcome in the first year of high attrition is a partial recouping of the funds; but in the second year, the base budget is likely to be cut to account for attrition. That is, in the second year the full $4,000 subsidy is removed because of increased attrition.

We began by saying that attrition seems to affect private institutions directly and quickly, and that public institutions seem to have more of a cushion. That observation is both true and false. Because the private institution has a better mix of funding sources, it can reallocate part of the funds if a student drops out. By contrast, the state institution usually has a very narrow range of funding sources; if it loses some funds, it may lose all of them. Incremental budgeting, however, does allow some cushion during the first year of a dropoff. Nevertheless, in the long run the full base of a public institution may be reduced and the impact of attrition may actually be much sharper than it is in a private institution.

In summary, a loss of students through attrition does not automatically cost either public or private institutions the full price of tuition immediately. Private institutions have a mix of funds that can be reallocated, and public institutions often have a cushion under incremental budgets. Nevertheless, in the long run the loss of the student will inexorably mean the full loss of either the tuition or the state subsidy. The only question is how long before this full impact is felt and how deep is the cushion that mitigates that impact.

Other Attrition Costs

Residence Halls and Auxiliary Services

Residence halls and other auxiliary services not only add to the breadth of a student's college experience but also contribute substantial revenues to the institution.

On-campus housing is the institution's largest nontuition revenue producer. On the average, students pay an additional $2,700 a year to live on campus. Therefore, a dormitory with a capacity for 800 students can generate up to $2,160,000 annually. Many residence halls, however, operate below maximum capacity. Even so, campus housing contributes a significant portion of revenue to the institution.

Historically, housing has gained and lost popularity cyclically. In the 1960s, many students refused to live in dorms, but in the late 1970s, waiting lists were substantial. Today, dormitories frequently run at or near capacity. If students drop out or move out early in the school year, the housing office can usually replace the residents with students from the waiting list. Most housing budgets are able to accommodate the fluctuations attributable to resident turnover. However, if a student drops out in the spring, the resident is more difficult to replace because once-interested students have already found housing elsewhere.

If replacements can be found for the residents that move out, the institution incurs fewer financial hardships. If, however, no replacements can be found and occupancy rates continue to drop, two serious financial consequences result. First, housing fees may go up to compensate for the lost revenue. Unfortunately, this may accelerate the drop in occupancy because the dorms will no longer be an inexpensive housing option. Instead, students will prefer the privacy of living in an apartment in the area for the same price. Second, in an effort to balance budgets, maintenance may deteriorate. This "undermaintenance" causes a decline in asset value, which is an unrecognized cost. According to Howard Bowen, physical assets such as the dormitory itself, the furniture, and the fixtures depreciate, and this depreciation is often not included in the institution's total operating expenses (Bowen, 1980). Similarly, when deferred maintenance—the failure to replace capital items—falls behind the rate of depreciation, these costs go unrecognized as well. Both of these factors, increased price and deteriorating physical maintenance, encourage further declines in on-campus residency. It becomes a vicious circle: as residents move out, revenue drops, facilities deteriorate, and more students are encouraged to move out.

Financially, the bookstore and campus food facilities are similar to dormitories. Like the dorms, other auxiliary services often defer maintenance when revenues decline. Deferred maintenance likewise leads to the deterioration of the facilities and to a reduction of quality service. A decline in quality discourages student use and further decreases the potential revenue produced by these campus facilities.

Higher Recruitment Costs

Although recruitment costs vary among institutions, estimates put the costs of recruiting a single student at between $200 and $800 (Finn, 1978). Sometimes, recruitment can cost half of a student's yearly tuition. Recruitment costs also vary among potential matriculants. The very students that cost the most to recruit—athletes, minorities—also have the highest attrition rates. The institution must increase its recruitment budget for these students with no guarantee that they will return the next year. The higher investment in each student is actually a risk that the institution takes; the college will lose that investment if the more expensive students leave in greater numbers.

The typical AASCU institution probably spends between $400 and $700 to recruit each new student. If recruitment falls short, increased retention can help take the heat off the admissions staff. Increased retention will also save the institution from higher recruitment costs in the future. On the other hand, if both recruitment and retention drop, the recruitment budget will likely be increased for the next year to make up for the loss. As the potential student cohort continues to shrink, it will become more expensive to recruit each single new student.

Dipping lower into the applicant pool and accepting more diverse students may also force the institution to expand academic support and student services to meet the needs of "nontraditional" students. Otherwise, colleges may be able to meet enrollment projections but will lose a high percentage of students by the end of the school year. Consequently, recruiters need to be aware of the long- and short-term results of their recruitment efforts. If high-risk, attrition-prone students are admitted, the college multiplies the risk of high attrition. Higher attrition will intensify recruitment demands, thus increasing the number of high risk students accepted. It's the vicious circle again: pressured recruitment leads to the acceptance of attrition-prone students who subsequently drop out, intensifying the recruitment problem even more.

Attrition hurts the college's public image, which in turn undermines recruitment. High attrition tarnishes the institution's image in two areas. High schools and alumni are two important constituencies that supply a constant stream of new students and community support. An institution's image needs to be favorable at the high-school level because of the extensive information grapeline that exists between present college students and the feeder high schools in the surrounding communities. When college students return to their high schools during semester breaks and convey bad impressions about a particular college, high schools will not remain feeder schools for long.

Alumni opinions are greatly valued because alumni supply the college with future students. They also donate money and provide services to the institution. If the alumni feel that the college has dropped in public esteem, they may decrease their support. Any decrease in alumni support will further perpetuate a college's negative image. Again, the vicious circle: attrition affects the public image of a college, which impairs potential recruitment from high schools in the area, decreases donor support, and thus contributes to a lower public image.

Programmatic Costs

A not-so-obvious consequence of extensive freshman attrition is an upper-division curriculum starved for faculty and students. An increased number of freshmen demand a larger number of faculty to teach introductory courses. Likewise, the upper division program can become limited and weak because the lower division dropouts are replaced largely by freshmen.

Departments that suffer high attrition will incur higher per student costs and budget cutbacks. Departments have differential costs. For example, a technical department with a highly tenured faculty, a low student/faculty ratio, and extensive equipment will have much higher costs than a social science department with a mix of tenured/nontenured faculty, a high student/faculty ratio, and low equipment costs. If enrollment drops in a department with high fixed costs, there will be serious financial consequences. First, the number of courses offered by the department will be reduced; second, no new equipment will be purchased; and third, program quality will diminish. Students will be discouraged from enrolling. Ironically, these students are the ones most needed to enroll to justify the program's existence and budget requests.

Michael Tierney's study, "Department Cost Functions" presents a financial evaluation of the costs of attrition for seven academic departments at thirty-one private liberal arts colleges (1980). Tierney cites the following example to illustrate how student attrition causes higher departmental costs per student.

A biology department has 150 FTE's at an average cost of $1,640 per student and marginal costs equal to $197 per student. If ten students drop out of the department, the department saves the marginal costs of the ten students ($197 X 10 = $1,970). However, if the marginal costs are subtracted from the total average costs of $246,000 ($1,640 X 150 FTE), the result is $244,030. When the remaining 140 FTE's are divided into this total departmental cost figure, the average cost per student is now $1,743! This is an increase of $103 per student! Hence, attrition causes higher, not lower instructional costs per student.

To summarize, attrition is expensive, and ongoing attrition may lead to various practices that further perpetuate attrition and financial instability. A vicious circle can develop in which the financial consequences of attrition actually encourage higher student dropout. The financial impact of attrition on the institutions is greater. Small decreases in enrollment cause a budget deficit. Small increases in an institution's retention rate can add literally thousands of dollars to a college's operating budget.

Institutional Strategies to Reduce Attrition

Institutions have little control over many of the factors that contribute to enrollment decline. Colleges have very little influence over the birth rate, the economy, draft policy, or public confidence in higher education. In contrast, colleges really can do something about their attrition rates.

To date, however, research reveals that most institutions have taken little effective action to reduce student attrition. In 1978 Vern Stadtman surveyed college presidents for the Carnegie Council (Stadtman, 1980); in 1979 a survey was done for the National Center for Higher Education Management Systems (Beal and Noel, 1980); and in 1971 we surveyed a national sample of both presidents and admissions directors. Table 10 reports the

Table 10: Campus Retention Strategies: The Results of Three National Surveys
(percentages)

Activity	Colleges Attempting the Activity		Colleges Reporting Activity Has Great Impact
	Stadtman (1980)	Beal and Noel (1980)	Baldridge, Kemerer, & Green (1982)
Orientation, Counseling and Advising	55	34	18
Career Planning	9	6	6
Learning Centers—Academic Support	36	24	29
Exit Interviews	9	3	2
Curricular Developments	13	2	6
New Policies—Grading Options	11	4	1
Improved Facilities	5	—	—
More Financial Aid	4	—	6
More Student/Faculty Contact	6	—	—
More Service to Nontraditional Students	3	—	8
Improved Student Activities and Services	7	—	—
Early Warning Systems	—	12	—
Peer Programs	—	4	—
Faculty/Staff Development	—	3	3
Multiple Action Programs	—	3	—
Cocurricular Activities	—	2	—
Dropout Studies	—	2	—
Improved Dorm Life	—	—	10

major conclusions from the three surveys. Several important trends emerge:

- All three surveys identified a long list of retention activities. But all three surveys revealed that only a handful of items have actually been tried by a significant number of institutions.

- Improved advising is clearly the option most often utilized. In fact, advising is mentioned more than all the other options combined in Stadtman's survey.

- Other efforts emphasize improving academic support programs, such as learning centers and remedial programs.

- Few institutions have attempted anything other than advising and some curricular changes.

- Most techniques are not judged effective.

It is apparent that most institutions have not done much in an attempt to lower their attrition rates. A major reason is that until recently most colleges have had such large recruitment pools that they have not needed coordinated and systematic programs to reduce attrition. This is a tragic oversight.

There are also *organizational* and *administrative* barriers to effective retention programs. For example, compare retention activities to recruitment efforts. From an organizational and administrative viewpoint recruitment is significantly different in that (1) it has a central administrative office, (2) success or failure is easy to evaluate, (3) resources (money, personnel, equipment) are clearly assigned, and (4) responsibility is highly centralized so that changes can be made directly by top managers. In short, recruitment is a centralized, focused, well-staffed, administrative function—and administrators can do something about it.

By contrast, retention has almost exactly opposite organizational and administrative characteristics. Who is in charge of retention? How do you evaluate the effort, and what administrators can be held responsible? Just how visible is the effort to the campus community? The answers to these questions suggest that retention efforts are decentralized, difficult to evaluate, not under the jurisdiction of a single administrator, understaffed, and under-budgeted. In short, retention efforts are an administrative night-mare, and they do not have a focal point. Nevertheless, every institution must now consider how to change this situation, how to have an impact on the retention problem.

Case Study One: A Consortium Effort

In 1981 the Kellogg Foundation of Battle Creek, Michigan, funded a consortium of eight southern California private institutions, working in coordination with the Higher Education Research Institute. The purpose of the consortium was to (1) assess the dimensions of the student dropout problem at the eight colleges, (2) plan strategies for cutting the attrition rate, (3) implement those strategies, and (4) evaluate the effectiveness of the program. The consortium has been exploring alternate strategies for reducing attrition. Out of all the strategies mentioned in the literature, the colleges have decided to implement new retention efforts in six areas.

Early Warning Systems

The traits of students who drop out have been extensively investigated. Armed with such information, the consortium's colleges hope to identify potential dropouts before students arrive on campus. The colleges will establish an "Early Warning System" to signal academic advisors and counselors when a student is showing signs of dropping out. Working with the admissions office, the retention task force on each campus is developing a list at the beginning of the freshman year of those students who are likely to drop out. Actually, the colleges have found the task surprisingly easy. Admissions officers can usually identify that segment of the freshman class that has dropout potential. In the past, admissions officers rarely set up such lists simply because no one asked for them. But on each of the consortium's campuses, the admissions office has been able to identify a dropout-prone segment of the freshman class.

What happens after the students are identified? The eight campuses are trying to provide a battery of special services: (1) high-intensity advising programs, with a handful of dropout-prone students attached to an advisor, (2) special attention to remedial academic programs for the dropout-prone segment, (3) early identification of poor academic performance, and (4) counseling programs for minority and nontraditional students.

The early warning system should result in more retention of the dropout-prone segment of the freshman class. Coupled with special services, an early warning system can short-circuit the deadly spiral of failure and social detachment that so often characterizes the student dropout.

Strong Residence Life and Social Integration

What are the colleges doing about the social integration issue? Thus far, the eight colleges in the consortium have taken the following steps:

- Major dormitory renovations are underway in three institutions.

- Five of the eight institutions are reconsidering their campus residency policies with an eye toward mandating more residential life.

- Most of the institutions are increasing their on-campus job possibilities, since one of the most consistent findings of the research is that on-campus jobs provide a focal point around which the student develops an integrated social life.

- Several campuses have spent extra money on intramural sports and other social activities.

The institutions believe that efforts to increase social integration and better social life on the campus will be rewarded handsomely in reduced attrition. Consequently, they have willingly invested in these efforts.

Curriculum Innovation to Reduce Attrition

A strong curriculum and an excellent faculty are the best retention tools a college can muster. By strengthening the academic program, and carefully meshing academic programs with student needs, retention will increase. This overarching goal, however, can too easily become a platitude without concrete effort to shape a responsive curriculum. The consortium's colleges are engaged in several innovative curricular activities.

First, most of the colleges have decided to increase funds and attention on remedial programs and learning skills centers. Most of the colleges have the same recruitment problems experienced by many other colleges—they are dipping lower into the applicant ability pool in order to admit enough students. The colleges have recognized the sad fact that more aggressive recruitment may actually increase the dropout rate and are making efforts to overcome it through learning skills centers, remedial courses, and early assessment of academic weaknesses for all entering students.

Second, the colleges have carefully examined their policies about academic majors. The literature suggests that students who do not declare an academic major early are more likely to drop (see Astin, 1977). These students are less likely to have clear academic goals or career objectives in mind. In addition, the higher dropout rate of undeclared majors may result because they are not integrated into the social and academic life of a department: they lack the careful advising and career counseling provided by the departmental faculty.

In the last decade or so, the emphasis of the curriculum swung toward more electives, more alternatives and less structure. Along with this curriculum flexibility came the lax attitudes on early declaration of a major. The consortium's colleges are now reconsidering those policies. Perhaps, some have posited, it would be better to have the students declare a major early and then make it easy to change majors if necessary. By contrast, a college that continues a policy of nondeclaration may wish to devote substantial energy to academic advising to encourage students to choose a major. Two consortium institutions consciously decided to continue a loose policy but substantially bolstered the support for undeclared students by adding better advising and intensive orientation programs. In any event, the colleges have given serious attention to their policy on choosing majors.

Third, in a further effort to bolster the academic program extended "orientation courses" have been developed for freshmen. In addition to the regular orientation program at the beginning of the year, several colleges have established a required semester-long freshman orientation course. The objective is to ensure that no freshman simply "floats" into the college without proper advisement or a strong peer group. The freshman orientation course has been used at half of the consortium's institutions, with great enthusiasm.

The Debate Over Advising

National surveys concerning attrition always arrive at the one strategy that is the most widely used: better advising. Consortium members have given much attention to advising. However, "better advising" has not been accepted as dogma. Many campus leaders actually felt that too much money and energy were being spent on advising systems, with too few results. The debate grew rather intense among consortium members. Many people believe that previous advising efforts—both through faculty and student services—had not been effective, and in some cases had been scandalously weak. The move to increase the *quality* of advising is at the top of the agenda for the colleges in the consortium, but there is a serious debate over how to accomplish the goal.

On the whole, most campuses feel that advising is vitally important, but that current practices simply are not living up to promised results. Consequently, many experiments have been proposed. One widely discussed strategy is the semester-long freshman course mentioned above. Several colleges decided to put money and personnel into such an orientation course rather than increase the resources of the traditional advising program. Other colleges are experimenting with the idea of a special "freshman dean," who would supervise freshman advising, especially in academic matters. And in all of the institutions there is increased concern about developing better advising programs for minorities and nontraditional students.

Focus on the Commuter Student

Commuter students are much more likely to drop out than are resident students. The consortium had previously invested very little energy to enriching the academic and social lives of commuter students. Although large amounts of money, student services, and programmatic effort had been directed toward resident students, little was allocated for commuter students. At the consortium institutions, like most institutions throughout the nation, the commuter student was essentially a second-class citizen. The consortium's colleges have now recognized this problem and are working to remove the stigma of the commuter student. In fact, the consortium compiled statistics to show that for most campuses a 10 or 12 percent improvement in the commuter dropout rate would provide a significant increase in retention for the entire institution.

One campus is building a new facility especially for commuter students; two campuses have opened up commuter-oriented wings in their existing student unions; two campuses have set up special budgets for social activities for commuter students; and several campuses worked hard to improve such basic services as parking and bookstore hours. Throughout the consortium, then, there has been renewed attention to the commuter students' plight and promise.

Linking Recruitment and Retention

When the consortium was formed, there was almost no link between admissions offices and the retention task forces. As time went on, however, it became obvious that improving retention was fundamentally a question of improving the match between student needs and institutional resources. To put it another way, effective retention grows out of effective recruitment. The better the match between the student and the institution, the higher the retention rate.

As the consortium developed its programs, the task forces quickly realized the significant link between recruitment and retention. Admissions directors became involved in retention task forces. Efforts were made on several fronts: (1) publications and advertisements were reviewed to make sure they accurately represented the academic and social life of the college, (2) admissions directors were involved in developing the "early warning systems" described earlier; (3) more attention was paid to assessing the special needs of low ability and nontraditional students; (4) "retention goals" were included in the enrollment planning of many colleges just as "recruitment goals" have always been. Good retention starts with good recruitment; all members of the consortium now understand and emphasize that link.

By late summer 1982, preliminary data from the eight campuses show substantial improvement in retention rates, particularly among freshmen. For example, one institution cut its freshman rate by 65 percent, going from twenty-six dropouts to nine. A second college, halved its freshman attrition by emphasizing residential life programs. A third college also reported substantial improvement in freshman retention rates largely because of its revised freshman advising program. A fourth campus estimates that improved retention has contributed approximately $130,000 in additional income.

Case Study Two: Bradley University

Bradley University, a private, largely undergraduate university of 5,500 students in Peoria, Illinois, suffered a serious enrollment shortfall in the early 1970s. To reverse the enrollment downturn, the university made various staff personnel changes and developed a new concept called "Student Planning." In 1977, the Student Planning concept was incorporated into a complete organization of student service units. The newly created Division of Student Planning linked the Office of Admissions, Office of Financial Assistance, Center for Orientation, Advisement, Retention, and Center for Career Development. In the process, attrition rates began to decline.

Bradley's Approach to Enrollment Management
Student affairs at Bradley is handled by two divisions in the Office of the Provost and Vice President for Academic Affairs: the student planning division and the student services division. The student services division consists of the deans of men and women, Counseling Center, Human Evaluation Center, Intramural Office, Health Center, Student Activities Office, International Student Services, and the Black Student Alliance. Since

there is no vice president for student affairs, student affairs is not separate from academic affairs.

The separation of student planning (admissions, financial assistance, orientation, advisement, retention, career development, and placement) from student services was intended to guarantee the former sufficient administrative attention to ensure its implementation. Because the student planning concept has total administrative support, the division's concerns (as well as those involving student services) are linked to the academic mainstream.*

Student planning has received sufficient personnel and economic support to launch comprehensive activities in several areas. The Office of Undergraduate Admissions maintains a heavy recruiting schedule, conducts an orderly plan of applicant flow research, and has an impressive array of recruiting literature at its disposal. The Office of Financial Assistance is well staffed and supported. Its role is critical within the student planning unit offering new student enrollment and retention support. The Office of Financial Assistance perceives its basic mission as being financial planning—offering short- and long-range financing options and assistance programs for all students, regardless of need.

The Center for Orientation, Advisement, and Retention

The Center for Orientation, Advisement, and Retention has developed an extensive repertoire of services. It conducts orientation programs for freshman and transfer students, as well as for parents. Brochures have been developed for each group on the theme "Right! . . . . . From the Start"; they emphasize the informal, personal dimension of Bradley University. Academic advisement is part of the orientation program. The center is responsible for administering the Academic Exploration Program (AEP), which assists academically undecided students. Staffed by center personnel, and some 30 volunteer faculty and administrative members, AEP annually serves as many as 900 students at one time. Its components include interest and preference surveys, self-assessment questionnaires, course sampling, and specialized advis-

---

* In July 1982, the two units were combined into one under the direction of the former head of the student planning division.

ing. A noncredit seminar, AEP 100, is also mandatory for undeclared students, emphasizing goal-setting, professional development, and self-concept and life-style consideration. Colorful full-size publications describing AEP are made available to all prospective students and their parents. The center also has an elaborate advising tool in the form of a cross-referenced index for AEP students and their advisors. This monograph, entitled *A Taxonomic Key for Academic Exploration Students and Their Advisors*, is designed to assist students to move in stair-step fashion from confusion and uncertainty to the selection of a major and determination of career objectives. The publication recently won a national award for excellence presented by the National Orientation Directors' Association.

The Student Aide Program

Another orientation/advising/retention tool is the Student Aide Program. Consisting of eight paid and trained undergraduate students, the Student Aide Program offers several important services, including:

*   *Bradley Connection:* student aides recruit over 300 volunteers annually from enrolled undergraduate students to provide prospective admitted students with information about the university. The Bradley Connection is thus part of the reinforcement phase in encouraging admitted students to enroll. Follow-up contact is provided when students enroll, and again at the start of a new academic year.

*   *Com-Link:* A computer-matching process that links student interests with campus clubs and groups that fit designated interests. Com-Link is used as an orientation device, as well as a retention tool, since it furthers student integration into campus life.

*   *Tutor-File:* A referral service linking students wanting special help with available tutors.

*   *Footsteps:* A career exploration program giving students an opportunity to investigate and test career interests by visiting with a professional for a day. After career interests have been

ascertained through appropriate testing and counseling, the student aides set up visits for enrolled students with professionals in Peoria, St. Louis, and Chicago having similar academic/career interests.

As part of its retention activities, the Center for Orientation, Advisement, and Retention regularly collects detailed information about campus climate (satisfaction-dissatisfaction) and the factors involved in student withdrawal decisions. The center also has developed a concerted "retention program" to reduce attrition, involving some of its services noted above. As a result of the ongoing study of attrition at Bradley, several important changes in campus routine have occurred. For example, the registration program was altered to allow for a lag between registration and the semester's start so that the university could better meet the demands of student interests by adding new class sections or increasing class enrollments. The time lag also allows the center to contact students who have not registered. The center works closely with the six colleges and academic departments to facilitate referrals from faculty members. Comparative statistics are made available to all university units showing the rate of attrition for the six colleges and for each academic department. Attrition data include breakdowns by such variables as grade point average (GPA), SAT scores, geographical origin, sex, and race.

Student retention efforts are not now, but likely will become a high priority with the faculty and administration. The healthy flow of new students into the university has deterred a concerted effort to improve student retention. Nonetheless, through administrative support and the dissemination of comprehensive retention information and data, certain programs and services are being revised and improved. Most notably, the university's system of academic advisement is being upgraded to provide students with more comprehensive guidance in academic and career-related areas. Likewise, deficiencies in nonacademic environments have been targeted for further study and improvement.

Results of Institution Efforts

In terms of enrollment, Bradley has recovered from the short-fall of the early 1970s, and thus can select a stronger calibre of student. Since 1975 Bradley has increased its applications for admission through 1981 by 49 percent; new student enrollment has increased by 21 percent; ACT test scores have moved from a composite of 21 to 23. Currently, 65 percent of entering freshmen graduate within four years, compared to 53 percent in the early 1970s. Fully 85 percent of freshmen stay at Bradley (comparative data for the early 1970s do not exist).

The attrition rates for AEP are traditionally high because AEP often serves as the last stop for students within declared major fields who are not doing well academically. Many academic departments require that students maintain a certain grade point average. If that level is not maintained, students are required to change to AEP and to search for a major in which they can find success. Likewise the Academic Review Board, in reinstating academically dismissed students, requires those students to re-enroll as undeclared in the AEP. This "clearinghouse" approach does, however, benefit AEP students by helping them make decisions, especially in the area of academic major selection. Once AEP students declare academic majors, only 6.1 percent make a second change. This compares to more than 60 percent of the student body in general who change their majors at least once.

Summary

It is apparent that colleges and universities are not doing all they can to reduce student attrition. This is particularly ironic, since retention is one aspect of enrollment management over which institutions can exert considerable control. This chapter has briefly reviewed the dimensions of the problem and presented some preferred strategies for dealing with it.

PART 2
THE CHALLENGE
OF INSTITUTIONAL VITALITY

Part One was concerned with specific practical steps that campuses can take to improve enrollment management. We discussed four issues: (1) initiating organizational changes to integrate student recruitment and retention activities with campus governance, (2) revitalizing the office of admissions, (3) linking recruiting and marketing, and (4) improving student retention.

Part Two is concerned with the broader issues of institutional quality and vitality. We do not believe in "quick-fix" solutions, in spite of our emphasis on practical, concrete issues. We want those practical issues to be viewed in the basic context of institutional quality, overall institutional health, and long-range organizational vitality.

Three arguments are made in Part Two. First, we suggest that planning approaches—essential to every institution facing enrollment uncertainty—should shift from conventional long-range planning to *strategic planning* (chapter six).

Second, we insist that every institution grapple with important mid-range "jugular vein decisions"—such as the link between student services and the faculty, personnel policies, and faculty governance. Such decisions are usually outside the realm of enrollment management but are so important that they have enormous indirect impact on enrollment matters (chapter seven). Third, we think that basic academic quality must be at the heart of every decision; quality must not be the victim of hurried attempts at solving enrollment problems (chapter eight).

Part Two is dedicated to the idea that effective enrollment management is, in the last analysis, a function of a high-quality, educationally effective institution.

CHAPTER 6
The Debate over Planning

As we saw in chapter one, predicting the future is risky. No one knows for certain whether we will have an enrollment crisis of major proportions or we will move through the eighties with only minor adjustments. Furthermore, overreaction to an expected problem can do as much damage as ignoring the problem entirely.

In the 1960s it seemed that enrollments would increase forever. This meant campuses had to expand and more Ph.D.'s had to be trained. But the planners overreacted. Physical plants were overbuilt and resources were overextended; now the spector of overcapacity haunts many administrators. Graduate programs were expanded; now the costly programs bleed the resources of many campuses. The supply of Ph.D.'s was increased; now many cannot find jobs. Hundreds of new colleges opened—one a week during the 1960s; now many institutions are threatened with closing because of declining enrollments.

Institutions may overreact again in the face of the expected enrollment crisis. There is reason to be concerned that faculty ranks may be needlessly reduced, that academic quality may be substantially undermined when institutions shift to part-time faculty, that expensive programs may be closed down only to be reopened later at enormous cost, and that the enrollment upturn predicted for the mid-1990s may catch many administrators off-guard.

Many institutions, prodded by state planning agencies, have begun to develop master plans for retrenchment. Much energy has been and is being expended on these large-scale plans—with mixed results. After examining the planning on numerous campuses, we have become convinced that many of these exercises are being conducted in a vacuum, divorced from campus realities.

Instead of vesting too much faith in grand plans, which may turn out to be wrong, institutions should seek the flexibility and dyamism that will allow adjustment to a number of alternative futures. If academic planners cannot easily predict the future, then they must develop the capacity to respond to uncertainty.

How can this flexibility be developed? In this chapter we will make two arguments:

• Traditional long-range planning has serious weaknesses on dealing with a rapidly changing and threatening environment.

• The emerging concept of "strategic planning" seems to hold definite promise.

In the process of examining each of these arguments, we will contrast traditional planning with strategic planning. Attention should be drawn here to a modified concept of long-range planning developed by AASCU's Resource Center for Planned Change. See especially *A Futures Creating Paradigm: A Guide to Long-Range Planning from the Future for the Future* (1978), described by Cameron Fincher as "a truly ambitious attempt at planning . . . which is tied to societal trends and value shifts that may take place within the institution's social, economic, and technological matrix." (Fincher, 1979). In the last part of the chapter we present a case study of Mercy College, an institution that carried through various strategic decisions and weathered handsomely the storm it faced.

The Weakness of Traditional Long-Range Planning

Organizations use long-range plans differently. In industry, corporate executives have become keenly interested in comparing the fit of day-to-day operations and profits with projected long-range market and profit goals, making adjustments where necessary. Other organizations, of which higher education institutions are prime examples, have often merely given lip service to the idea of long-range planning.

Master plans flourished in higher education at mid-century. By the end of the 1960s almost every educational institution or system and state government had some instrument or group of instruments that could be labeled a "master plan" (Glenny, Shea, Ruyle, and Freschi, 1976). At that time, of course, these master plans were drawn to deal with rising enrollments and to ensure some orderliness in the expansion and growth of new programs and new campuses.

As education moved from the growth and expansion of the 1960s to the constrictions of the 1970s and 1980s, these master plans often failed to deal with the complexities of the changing environment. In the course of our case study interviews and our studies of college administrations we invariably encountered evidence that long-range planning in higher education has had limited success and effectiveness.

General Disillusionment with Planning

Answers to our questions about planning activities on college campuses give a fair idea of the disillusionment of participants in long-range planning. Planning practices are often dubbed "meaningless" and "a waste of time." Respondents said that "events are so unpredictable it is impossible to plan effectively," or "the process is so complicated and time-consuming, we don't have the time to deal with it." Others commented: "Yes, we do a lot of planning around here, and we even have a master plan for the college. We don't use it very much and most of its predictions are wrong. But we have one in case the trustees ask."

Or this: "Sure we have a master plan. It is essentially a cut-and-paste job. Every academic department wrote up a wish list and then we slapped them all together between two covers. It doesn't have much relationship to the budget, and frankly, nobody pays much attention to it."

The following themes run through our interviews: (1) the process is so lengthy and complicated that planning loses its meaning, (2) the process becomes more important than the results, and (3) the plan does not make any sense to those who are actually doing the work because it is rarely linked to daily operations and to the budget. It would be naive to think that the planning process could not be made simple and less time-consuming. Often planners make the process more complicated than is necessary for obtaining effective results. Models depicting elaborate stages and steps capture the fancy of theorists but become impractical for those trying to operationalize the process sensibly.

Specific Problems in Planning

The gap between the plan and the budget is common to both universities and industry (Hobbs and Heany, 1977). This failure to link planning with operational activities was illustrated in the reply of a university vice president to the question, "How do you see the connection between what your office does and the long-range planning of the university?" After a rather lengthy pause, came the reply, "The Board of Trustees is responsible for the long-range planning, we don't have anything to do with it. It is completely a separate thing." Our interviews with department chairpersons and faculty revealed that for the most part these individuals had little or no input into long-range planning and, furthermore, saw little connection between what went on in their departments and the work done by the planning office or the board of trustees. The general attitude was "they do their job and we do ours."

The frequent turnover of top administrators in higher education constitutes another problem that affects institutional planning. Continuity in the planning process is disrupted by the arrival of new administrators. They bring their own frame of reference and sometimes appoint their own staffs; previous plans are often discarded as the new era begins. This is particularly apt to occur when institutional problems are serious and a new administration is ushered in to resolve them. The new regime is likely to prove very discouraging to those who have invested time and effort in previous planning attempts. If a college has had several presidents in a short time, which is not unusual, the faculty's attitude becomes "so here we go again." The *deja vu* syndrome contributes to general lassitude toward institutional planning.

In one case study situation, the president's task force on planning and budgeting had worked on a project for two years. Their stated purpose was to develop a procedure which would produce good planning and tie planning to the budgeting of resources. A number of documents were developed, including a statement of the university's planning assumptions, a statement of the university's mission, and a step-by-step planning procedure. A pilot process was tested on twenty departments of the institution. The task force worked hard to involve faculty representatives from various academic areas, but when the process was ready for implementation there was a change in the presidency of the school. The process was halted, the project was discarded, and the planning system was not referred to again.

To summarize, these are some major stumbling blocks to effective planning:

• Planning processes are complicated and time-consuming.

• There is a gap between planners at the top administrative level and planners on the operational level.

• Frequent turnover of executives disrupts the planning process.

• Budgets are poorly linked to plans.

The Key Failure of Planning:
Mismatch with Administrative Behavior

The last major criticism of traditional long-range planning is that the behavior of administrators as described in planning models simply does not correspond with the way administrators actually work.

Planning models are very clear about how administrators *ought* to behave. A good administrator, according to the theorists, should be oriented to long-range efforts and impacts, should set goals clearly and crisply, should organize efforts so that the goals are accomplished and evaluated, should avoid short-term crisis-oriented reactions, and should be highly "rational" in assessing the facts relevant to a decision. Deliberate behavior is the ideal to which every administrator should aspire—at least that is the basic theory. (For examples of these emphases in the literature, see Peterson, 1980; Cosand, 1980, Fenske, 1980.)

By contrast, most administrators are ineffective when compared to the ideal. They certainly do not describe their behavior the way the planners insist they should. In fact, interviews with administrators reveal a rather shocking ineptitude, at least by planners' ideals. They often report that their lives are crisis-oriented, moving from one event to the next with little time for long-range planning.

Most importantly, these administrators seem never to clarify their goals or line their objectives up neatly with goals. Administrators often seem to be wandering around in a bewildering maze of conflicting, constantly changing objectives.

Moreover, despite the emphasis on program evaluation over the last decade, real-world administrators often report that they rarely make decisions about program continuation based on rational evaluation. What little evaluation is actually done is usually highly political in character, focusing on the support a program can muster from various interest groups rather than on a rational evaluation of merit.

Finally, even when the busy administrator finally makes a plan, rarely is it executed! People often do not follow it and staff turnover frequently dates the plan before it can be implemented. In short, the picture of real-world administration simply does not jibe with the ideal of planning theorists.

Either the harrassed administrators are performing poorly or the planning theorists are wrong, their theories unrealistic, and their abstract concepts in need of revision.

Administrators would defend themselves by arguing that the real world does not neatly fit the theories of planners. Planners would respond by saying, "Yes, we understand that things do not work like our theories suggest. However, you *ought* to try to work this way. If you did, administrative effectiveness would improve."

Which is right, the administrator's *description* of the real world or the planner's goal of improving administrative behavior? We believe the theories should be adjusted to reality, not the reverse. What is needed is a theory that addresses administrative practice rather than demands that a zebra change its stripes. If real-world administrative behavior is crisis-oriented, then what is needed is a better theory of crisis management. If goals are really complex, ambiguous, and contested, then what is needed is a decision theory that handles goal complexity instead of demanding goal simplicity. If administrative thinking is oriented toward the short- rather than the long-term, then what is needed is a

theory to improve short-term decisions so that long-term out-
comes improve. If real-world administration is highly political as
well as rational, then what is needed is a theory for improving
political skills. In short, the theory should relate to the real world.

The literature of recent years reflects a growing understanding of a number of important issues. In particular, the attempts to
understand the nonrational area of decision making has been
substantially advanced by the research and writing of James G.
March (see especially Cohen and March, *Leadership in Ambiguity,*
1976). At the same time, several important books have been
written on the subject of political approaches to decision-making,
most notably the excellent book by Graham Allison (*The Essence
of Decision,* 1971) and the texts of J. Victor Baldridge (*Power and
Conflict in the University,* 1971 and *Policy Making and Effective
Leadership,* 1978). All these attempts to formulate alternative
models of decision-making that more realistically match actual
administrative behavior cannot be explored here. Instead we will
focus on only one new approach, one expounded in the strategic
planning literature, that offers a promising alternative to conventional long-range planning.

The Development of Strategic Planning in Higher Education

What is strategic planning? What are its intellectual origins?
How is it different from traditional long-range planning? The
central focus of strategic planning is developing a good fit between
an organization's activities and the demands of the environment
around it. Strategic planners look at the big picture—the long-
range destiny of the institution, the competition between an
organization and others in its environment, the market for organizational products and services, and the mix of internal resources to accomplish the organization's purpose. Strategic planning emphasizes flexibility and quick response to changes in the
outside environment. Its basic perspective is external—looking
toward the environment around the organization—rather than
internal—looking at the organization's structure. The goal of
strategic planning is not so much producing plans as making
critical decisions wisely. It is not so much interested in doing

things right as it is in doing the right things. Effectiveness, not efficiency, is the watchword of strategic planning.

Of course, good decision makers in complex organizations have always acted this way, long before anyone coined the term "strategic planning." Recently, however, writers in business schools and management centers have been trying to develop a more coherent description of the strategic management process.

Strategic Planning in Higher Education

Robert Cope has recently written a book, entitled *Strategic Planning, Management, and Decision Making,* in which he reviews the development of the strategic planning literature and examines its application to American higher education (Cope, 1981). Cope comments on the intellectual roots of strategic planning:

> *The ideas and techniques of the strategic view are developing from a convergence of several disciplines and subdisciplines. The clearest connection is with schools of management from which policy, marketing, and effectiveness research is being adapted for use in higher education. Policy research is aimed at determining the nature of the activity in which the organization is to engage and what kind of organization it is to be. Marketing helps determine more directly what the organization's current and probable clients want. Effectiveness research seeks to determine what combination of organizational policies and need fulfillment results in success. The literature about policy, marketing, and effectiveness overlaps and converges in strategic planning. Nearly all of this literature has developed in the last 15 years in the management schools and has been applied to higher education for only about 3 years. (Cope, 1981, p. iv.)*

In many ways, strategic planning is a state of mind rather than a planning technique. The word "strategy" is basically a military term, and a military analogy might help explain the focus of strategic planning.

Strategic Planning: A Military Analogy

Assume that an army wanted to mount a major invasion, such as the American and British armies did on D-Day in Normandy. What would they do about planning? Clearly, the first move would be to develop plans for conducting the invasion. It is easy to imagine office buildings full of generals, admirals, and planning staffs drawing up attack plans, logistical requirements, and transportation needs. Undoubtedly these people would be doing conventional long-range planning. They would lay out budgets and assemble the necessary armaments and men, analyze the need for new equipment and order its production, lay out terrain maps and specify how troops would move across it, and set up a chain of command. In short, they would do many things we typically associate with traditional planning.

But what happens when the invasion is launched? Everyone knows that the original plans will almost certainly falter, that parameters will change, and that the rapidly changing military environment will upset and unravel plans made in office buildings far from the front.

The military unit going into battle undoubtedly will have a master plan. But its real success will rest on adequate response to changing conditions, on flexibility in meeting new demands, and on internal strength that allows rapid redeployment. As every good military commander knows, no matter how carefully the plans have been made, the actual battle will take a different turn.

Knowing this fact, a strong battle commander builds a response capacity. Troops are assembled with elements of redundancy built in so extra strength is available for every move. Complex efforts are undertaken to scan the environment: intelligence networks are built to ferret out the enemy's movements; reconnaissance efforts are mounted to find out where the original plans went astray and by how much. Elaborate communications are structured so the commander can monitor the situation and rapidly deploy forces for new moves. Strategic reserves are held back so that fresh forces can be thrown into the rapidly changing situations when they are needed. And contingency plans are developed to provide alternatives if the original fails. In short, the battlefield requires a decidedly different mind set and a much different set of behaviors. The successful commander must be quick, know when to adapt the original plans to the changing realities, constantly scan the battlefield environment, and respond rapidly with critical decisions.

We are arguing that the leaders of American higher education must learn to think more like the battlefield commander than the desk top planner back at headquarters. Unfortunately, most planning models were designed for headquarters; the strategic planning literature tries to reorient the discussion toward the battlefield.

Some people will argue that a battlefield analogy is inappropriate for higher education—in fact, people *have* argued this in seminars where we have discussed strategic planning. Nevertheless, this analogy clearly helps to establish the strategic perspective, and to highlight the contrast between strategic planning and conventional long-range planning.

Let us emphasize here that we are *not* suggesting that conventional long-range planning be discarded. Long-range planning is still necessary to bring about rational change in organizational life. What we are suggesting is that campus administrators need to be concerned with short-range concerns as well, just as battlefield commanders do. Strategic planning provides the means to adjust long-range plans to changed circumstances.

The Major Emphases of Strategic Planning

In this section we will try to draw out in more precise form the distinctions between conventional long-range planning and the emerging theory of strategic planning (see also Kotler and Murphy, 1981).

The Organization's Destiny. Strategic planning asks the basic questions of institutional health and survival. In fact, much of the early work in strategic planning focused on businesses that were either spectacular successes or spectacular failures! Both ends of the continuum were interesting because they showed how strategic planning was related to the institutions' vitality and survivability.

The Task of Top-Echelon Managers. Usually the only people with enough power and enough perspective to make decisions about the institution's destiny, its role in society, and its competition with other organizations are top managers. Business literature, in particular, tends to view strategic planning as a task for this level of decision-maker. Robert Cope, however, challenges this view, arguing that educational institutions are more democratic, more professionalized, and more influenced by the voice of faculty and students (Cope, 1981). Consequently, he suggests that in higher education strategic planning should be the task not only of top managers, but of all institutional participants. We agree with Cope and believe that people throughout the institution *ought* to be involved in the discussion of strategic issues. Nevertheless, in the real world most major strategic decisions require the exercise of extensive power and are invariably made by top-echelon decision-makers.

Time Orientations in Strategic Planning. Conventional planning asserts that plans must extend out far into the future. The reality is that such plans are apt to fail because environmental conditions change so rapidly. It is not uncommon to find colleges and universities with documents called five-year or ten-year plans; it *is* uncommon to find anybody using such documents in day-to-day decision making.

By contrast, strategic planning relies on rapid assessment of the environment and on decision-making that grapples with short-term and medium-range issues. The emphasis is on·doing the right thing today, so that in the long run, the organization will be better off. This does not mean that people using strategic planning models ignore the future; it simply means that they tend to be more modest in their time frames and understand the long-term impacts of today's decisions.

Sensitivity to Organizational Environment. Most factors that determine the organization's long-range destiny originate in the outside environment. Higher education in the last decade has been brutally awakened to the significance of environmental forces, for example, substantial demographic shifts in the student recruitment pools, coupled with a shake up in governmental financial support.

Conventional long-range planning tends to rely on a "closed system" model; strategic planning, however, is an "open system" model. The focus is on assessing the turbulent environment surrounding a college or university. Strategic planning examines such issues as market segmentation, interorganizational competition, interaction with funding agencies, and the matching of the environment's needs with the organization's capabilities. The strategic planner knows the importance of developing a range of alternate scenarios and back-up positions as contingencies for a changed environment. Unlike the traditional planner, the strategic planner is outward looking. This fundamental reorientation of perspectives is probably the single most important contribution that the strategic planning literature brings to higher education management.

Strategic Planning as an Art. Proponents of traditional long-range planning argue that there is a "management science" for the planning enterprise that requires rationality, quantatative analysis, and highly technical planning techniques.

By contrast, advocates of strategic planning see it as an art form—a subtle blend of facts, hunches, assessments, experiences, and experiments. Both qualitative judgments and quantitative analyses are blended in a strategic planning effort. In particular, the experienced judgments of professional faculty are seen as important to a strategic planner's decision process.

Stream of Decisions in the Strategic Process. The long-range planner sees a *plan* as the capstone of his efforts, a blueprint for the action that is supposed to guide the organization. The strategic planner, in contrast, sees the capstone effort to be a *stream of decisions* that help move the organization into the future. The long-range planner is usually concerned with producing the *right* plan in view of the facts, figures, and crystallized goals. The strategic planner, on the other hand, is much more interested in making a *wise* decision that is the subtle blend of qualitative and quantitative matters. Good college administrators, we believe, do not blanch at the thought of making wise decisions.

A stream of critical decisions instead of a plan and a blueprint, an emphasis on "wise" decisions instead of "right" decisions, an orientation to effectiveness rather than efficiency, an eye toward doing the right thing instead of doing things right—these shifts in meaning and perspective characterize the strategic planning approach (see Table 11).

Mercy College: Strategic Planning at Work

All the evidence suggests that small private liberal arts colleges will be the institutions most threatened by enrollment difficulties, and the Northeast will be the most vulnerable geo-

Table 11: Comparison of Strategic Planning and Conventional Planning

Activity	Strategic Planning	Conventional Planning
Arena of Planning	Organization's destiny, market	Wider range of issues, nonroutine and routine
Who Plans	Top-level officials	Planning office
Time Orientation	Medium/short-range	Long-range
System Perspective	External, environmental	Internal, organizational
Theoretical Perspective	Open system	Closed system
Decision Data	Both quantitative and qualitative	Quantitative
Decision Process	Complex art form	Exact science
Outcome	Stream of critical decisions	Plan, blueprint

graphic area. Yet in spite of these dire forecasts, one college has prospered in the face of such predictions, expanding its enrollment and programs through aggressive action. Let us examine the strategic decision Mercy College made to accomplish this turnaround. (Note: the SUNY-Potsdam case study in the next chapter provides another example of planning at the campus level.)

Mercy College grew from an enrollment of 1,500 in 1972 to over 9,500 students enrolled in day, evening, and weekend sessions in 1981. This phenomenal growth in just a decade was due primarily to changes in directorship, philosophy, and mission that converting the school from a small, all-female, Catholic college to an expanding, coeducational, nonsectarian institution. The philosophy and personal administrative style of the man who led Mercy College through this traditional period to its current status is of particular interest.

A Shift in Institutional Mission

Mercy College, whose main campus is located in Westchester County, New York, began as a Catholic junior college in 1950 under the auspices of the Sisters of Mercy. The original mission of the school was to train nuns to teach in grammar schools. As the number of nuns decreased in the Catholic church during the 1960s, the college increasingly admitted lay women. In 1961 the institution became a four-year college offering academic programs leading to the baccalaureate degree.

In 1969 the Sisters of Mercy decided to relinquish the college, which no longer served the mission for which it was founded. The college was turned over to a lay board and became nonsectarian and coeducational. Eligibility for participation in the state funding programs for private institutions was a major impetus for the decision for Mercy College to assume nonsectarian status. In 1972 Don Grunewald was appointed as the college's first permanent lay president, and under his leadership the institution grew and expanded.

Strategic Decision: "Take the Campus to the Students"

The first major strategic decision was to drop all pretext of being a small residential college and to shift to a service orientation for commuting students. There was gradual emergence and expansion of summer, evening, and weekend sessions, and of offerings in bilingual and adult education. The college opened a branch campus in Yorktown Heights and offered courses at a variety of other sites in the metropolitan area. Today, there are extension centers in Peekskill, White Plains, Yonkers, and the Bronx. In addition, courses are offered at six correctional facilities. And, since 1975, the Brooklyn Center of Long Island University has offered graduate courses on the Mercy College campus.

All academic offerings are available at each location, making the educational processes more convenient and accessible to students from the New York metropolitan area. Programs are offered in liberal arts and sciences and professional studies; the college grants the Bachelor of Arts, Bachelor of Science, Associate in Arts, and Associate in Science degrees. Also offered are career-oriented certificate programs in a variety of areas.

Mercy College draws students from Westchester County and the New York/New Jersey/Connecticut metropolitan areas. Eighty percent of the students live within four miles of the campus. There are approximately 200 students from foreign countries, the largest group being from Nigeria; and the largest minority groups are Blacks and Hispanics, who constitute about 20 percent of the total student population. The average age of the student is approximately 27 years, and there is roughly the same percentage of male and female students.

The President's Entrepreneurial Style

Mercy does not have a clearly defined, formal approach to planning that structurally attempts to include a wide representation of ideas. (The SUNY-Potsdam case study in the next chapter provides an interesting contrast.) And the Board of Trustees does not appear to play an active role in long-range planning. At Mercy, the key figure is the president, whose personable and entrepreneurial approach tries to anticipate the needs of both traditional and nontraditional student markets.

President Grunewald holds bachelor's and master's degrees in history, but his doctorate is from the Harvard School of Business and his experiences prior to his appointment at Mercy included academic administration. During our interviews with Grunewald, it was very apparent that he takes a personal interest

in every aspect of the college. He exuded an aura of proud owner-
ship of every building and every piece of equipment on the campus. His easy familiarity with all the activities and programs of
the college, coupled with his apparently congenial relations with
faculty and staff indicated an individual very much in control of
the organization and enjoying the personal touch he gives to it.

Monitoring the Environment

President Grunewald's approach to planning is strategic—
he constantly monitors the environment and calculates how Mercy
College can respond to trends, changes, and needs. Aside from
the once nontraditional, but now accepted, programs like the
weekend college, Mercy has also tried some novel approaches
to meeting student needs which, in Grunewald's estimation,
"have worked." One is parallel scheduling: the same courses are
given by the same faculty member both in the morning and
evening. Parallel scheduling is helpful to students who work
shifts, which is not unusual in the Westchester County area. If
the shift changes, the student may switch from the morning to
the evening class, or vice versa, without "going through any red
tape."

Another approach is to tie in financial aid with scheduling.
This is accomplished by offering two courses in each 8-week
session during the long term. The student can then register
for four courses in a semester and be eligible for financial aid,
but take only two courses concurrently. Mercy College uses
every opportunity to offer a variety of courses. A one-month
intersession is offered in January between the long semesters as
well as usual summer sessions. The college tries to respond quickly
to student demand: if "Mohammed can't come to the mountain,
you take the mountain to Mohammed." Courses are taught at
extension centers and in correctional institutions. The scope of
the college's approach is well illustrated by the computer sessions it offered for children in the summer of 1981. These were
taught by the college faculty. Grunewald's idea was to "get the
kids used to coming to Mercy and having fun with these courses."

Maintaining Flexibility

All college properties except the one main campus are rented.
This provides for more flexibility. If more space and facilities

are needed, Mercy College rents them. If less space is needed, the college does not have "to sell or waste; just don't lease." By renting, the college goes to where the market is. If one area is losing students and not doing well, another location is considered.

The same contingent and strategic thinking is applied to academic programs. A number of associate degree and certificate programs are offered at Mercy. Students, particularly adults, are recruited for these programs and, once enrolled, are encouraged to continue for four years. Essentially a four-year college, Mercy College nonetheless makes provision for programs that do not lead to a bachelor's degree. Whenever feasible, associate degree programs are offered in the same fields of study as in the four-year program. The college has currently applied to the state of New York for an Associate Degree in Secretarial Science and Graphic Arts, programs intended to attract students who will ultimately enter the four-year programs in these areas.

Because Mercy has thus far been unable to get state approval to offer graduate programs, the college took an alternative route. Long Island University was approached to give courses on the Mercy College campus. Since 1975, Mercy has done most of the recruiting for Long Island's graduate program, and most of the teaching is done by the Mercy College faculty. Long Island University gives the degree; and the two institutions share revenues after expenses.

Recently Mercy College applied for a master's program in nursing: another strategy in attempting to gain approval to offer graduate programs. The college currently offers an upper division program for those who are already registered nurses. According to the president, Mercy applied for a graduate program in nursing rather than any other area because this is the only program that has any likelihood of being approved, and once Mercy has a bona fide program on the graduate level, it hopes to offer more. Thus, even though the nursing program would be costly to the institution, it would be worth it. President Grunewald sees this as a way of "getting a foot in the door, and being ready to accept the costs."

Institutional Accomplishments

In 1972 when Grunewald became president, succeeding a lay acting president, the college had an enrollment of 1,500, approximately 70 percent of whom were women. One-half of the department chairpersons and less than 55 percent of the faculty had doctorates. The college owned one building and classes were offered on the one campus. The library holdings totalled 60,000 volumes, and the only career programs offered were teacher training and medical technology.

Today, the college has an enrollment of 9,400 with an additional 800 students in a graduate program affiliated with Long Island University. All department chairpersons and 60 percent of full-time faculty have doctorates. There are two campuses and four extension centers, and courses (mainly lower division and some remedial) are being offered at six correctional facilities. The main library houses a total collection of 280,000 volumes, as well as extensive audiovisual materials.

Career programs include business administration, criminal justice, education, computer-information science, medical technology, nursing, public safety, and social work. The college will soon be offering a program in veterinary technology management, a four-year program to educate individuals to function as assistants to veterinarians and to work in veterinary laboratories. This program is the first of its kind to be offered. Mercy's Weekend College draws interested students in business administration, criminal justice, behavioral science, and computer science. Continuing education programs were started a year ago, and Dr. Grunewald anticipates that these, too, will grow. Figure 7 depicts graphically the upward trend in student course registrations at Mercy College between 1974 and 1981.

Comments on Strategic Planning at Mercy
The administration at Mercy College is highly centralized and typifies "benevolent autocracy." Grunewald is very much in control of the institution and is the key architect of the growth, expansion, and direction for Mercy. The president's personal philosophy is to provide educational opportunities in as many ways as possible to as many in the community who need or desire them. It is this vision and challenge that led to the development of new programs and new approaches to looking at old problems. President Grunewald's background in business administration and his own knowledge of the community, gained from growing up

Figure 7. Student Course Registration by Session,
All Locations and All Departments
(registration figures in thousands)

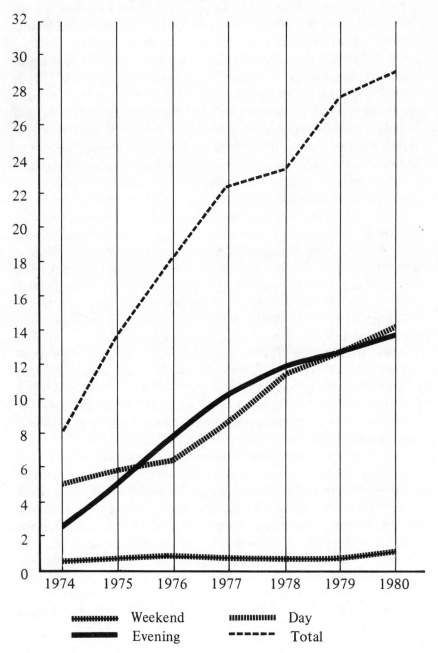

in Westchester County, provide him with the proper preparation for carrying out this mission.

While exercising his formal authority as chief executive officer of Mercy, Grunewald also creates an organizational climate that encourages the generation of creative ideas from his administrative officers and faculty. At Mercy College this has led to a mode of thinking that may be described as "contingency-strategic." "If not this, then what?" seems to be a question that is perpetually asked. Answering that question involves constant monitoring of both the internal and external environments and maintaining flexibility within the educational system. His beliefs in leasing, rather than purchasing, facilities and in holding regular informal "brainstorming" sessions with his administrative officers provide the mechanisms for institutional flexibility to respond to environmental changes.

Whether President Grunewald's administrative style creates loyalty to the institution among the faculty is not readily answerable. We can only note that faculty turnover at Mercy College is very low despite the fact that Westchester County is an expensive area and faculty salaries at Mercy are lower than those in the state system. Too, faculty schedules are demanding. Because Mercy attempts to meet student needs, faculty are expected to teach at two locations, and both morning and evening classes are part of their regular load. During the first year of Grunewald's presidency, the faculty attempted to unionize. The union vote resulted in a tie, and since then no further attempts have been made. The question that comes to mind is whether faculty would continue to be satisfied with these working conditions under a different type of leadership?

Mercy's growth and expansion in a period when many higher education institutions are undergoing decline in enrollment is difficult to understand. Whenever an entrepreneurial approach is effective in increasing enrollment, the question of quality is bound to arise. Grunewald acknowledges that this is a problem that the college has had to deal with constantly. In attempting to provide a variety of educational opportunities to a wide variety of students, maintenance of standards often conflicts with the desirability of giving individuals "a chance."

Internally, a variety of approaches to maintaining quality have been tried. By his own admission, the president during his first year, "pressured the faculty who gave everyone an A, and the word quickly got around." Now, each department monitors its own standards, and the dean's office provides a measure of control. All final grades are posted 'publicly so everyone may see how grades compare from department to department and from course to course. Because the same courses are taught by different faculty on a variety of campuses, most departments now use common syllabuses, the same textbooks, and several forms of standard examinations. This is especially true in the basic courses in English and mathematics. Group grading is another approach that has been tried in an attempt to control quality. An appeals process exists for both faculty and students if there are any complaints of unfair grades. One other approach for controlling quality is through keeping the class sizes manageable. The student/faculty ratio at Mercy College is 16:1.

Lessions to be Learned

What can be learned from the Mercy case study? Several points are important:

- *Environmental monitoring* is necessary, for it can help match the institution's services with the market's demands.

- A key factor in this institution's growth and development is *administrative leadership.* An administrator providing a strong, stable, and enthusiastic leadership enables the college to establish itself as an expanding and independent educational force in the community. Mercy College is committed to providing a variety of educational opportunities to both traditional and nontraditional students, and in keeping with this philosophy, has made no attempt to develop an "elitist" image so frequently pursued by private schools.

- An *organizational climate* encourages flexibility and leads to a contingency-strategic mode of thinking. Generating creative ideas for program development and new approaches to traditional practices in keeping with environmental changes and trends is congruent with today's concepts of strategic planning in organizations.

- *Problem areas* need to be monitored continually. The institution must maintain both quality as well as quantity if it is to
  remain viable and effective. Too, there is the issue of effective leadership, if and when administrative changes occur.

Summary

To conclude this chapter let us review our major points.
First, we have suggested that traditional planning models are
not likely to be as helpful as its proponents usually suggest.
While formal long-range planning provides the perspective necessary to study alternative institutional futures and to set the stage
for major institutional change, it is not responsive to rapid environmental developments. Long-range planning needs to be
adapted to the real world within which colleges and universities
function. The addition of a strategic planning capacity enables
this to be done.

Strategic planning focuses on the organization's destiny
with particular reference to its place in the external environment.
Constituency, market, and competition are salient features of the
strategic mentality. Usually strategic planning is seen as a function
of key executives rather than an activity lodged in a staff planning
office. It has several other features: it's time perspective is medium
or short-term, it uses an open system instead of a closed system
approach, and it utilizes both qualitative and quantitative information in a process that is more an art form than a science. The key
objective of strategic planning is a stream of wise decisions rather
than a plan or a blueprint that can be forgotten. As an example of
how such planning can be adopted and succeed, the case study
of Mercy College was presented.

CHAPTER 7

The Focus on
Strategic Decisions

We mentioned in chapter six that the key outcome of strategic planning is a stream of decisions, not a blueprint or plan for making decisions. Many of these decisions are closely related to enrollment management; in this chapter we broaden the discussion to look at several of them.

The Concept of "Jugular Vein" Decisions

During the research for this book we interviewed the provost of a large university who used the phrase "jugular vein" decisions. He contrasted them to the activities of the master planners, the group that was trying to plan for his institution's future five or ten years out, and offered this comment:

> I am more than happy to let my enemies run the long-range planning committees. They are off in the corner running their statistical projections, devising their 'mission statements.' and making up their master plans. In the meantime, I am doing the unimportant stuff—at least from their point of view. I am setting the budgets, selecting the key people, and funding key programs. I call these the jugular vein decisions. In the long run I am positive that I will have more influence over this institution's future. The staff I select and the funding decisions I make will outmaneuver the grand planners with their schemes and statistics.

This provost was probably correct. The medium-range decisions about budget, staffing, and major problems will determine at least as much about the institution's destiny as the master plans. These strategic or "jugular vein" decisions build the institution's infrastructure and its flexibility for an uncertain future. As noted in chapter six, we obviously must have long-range plans and planners, but those plans must have built-in flexibility that will sustain institutions when the planners are wrong.

Examples of "Jugular Vein" Decisions

What are "jugular vein" decisions? The following list contains some examples:

- *Implementing major budget changes:* Most budgeting is certainly not "zero-based" in spite of the promotion of this model in recent years. Instead, a budget is largely a minor, incremental adjustment of the allocation from the previous year. However, when substantial budget changes can be made to emphasize new priorities, programs, or constituent demands, these changes become opportunities for important decisions.

- *Selecting key faculty and administrators:* Nothing shapes an institution like the quality of its people. One president we interviewed stated it simply: "The most important thing I've done in the past six years has undoubtedly been the selection of the key deans. Nothing else even comes close in terms of the impact that these decisions have."

- *Shaping the relationship to the outside environment:* Top administrators must constantly be looking outward at the world and inward at the organization. Several environmental questions trigger "jugular vein" decisions: What are the basic demographics of the region, such as population, migration, and age distribution? What is our client pool and how can we best tap it? What other organizations compete with us, and how do we interact with them? Who are the key funding sources and what is our relationship to them? What is the political context and how is it changing?

- *Influencing key policies:* In every college or university a handful of institutional policies shapes the institution's destiny—admissions policies, collective bargaining contracts, affirmative action mandates, promotion and tenure policy, and graduation requirements. Administrators often feel that shaping these policies is routine work, an activity frequently handed over to middle-level staff people. This is a significant mistake because these policies will guide the institution for a long time. Unless these policies are especially well-crafted, they will limit an institution's adaptability. Unfortunately, administrators do not often think that policy-making is important because it is rarely as exciting as confronting crisis situations. Nevertheless, shaping important *policies* is a critical "jugular vein" decision and should not be neglected.

Building more effective organizational systems: Although the organizations are usually well-structured and rarely require significant changes, administrators occasionally have an opportunity to make them. Examples of "system building" strategic decisions: adding another school, college, or division; eliminating major program sets; building a management information system; shaking up the organizational hierarchy; or constructing a better linkage to outside organizations. (See chapter two regarding reorganization for improved enrollment management.)

These decisions share common features: they are medium-term, can usually be controlled at the local campus, are within the span of influence of key administrators, and have important consequences. Although hardly an exhaustive list, such matters can be classified as strategic or "jugular vein" decisions.

Three Sets of Strategic Decisions

The remainder of this chapter will examine case studies and survey data involving three important strategic decisions: attempts to build viable faculty governance to identify institutional priorities in case of cutbacks, analyses of changing personnel practices in response to anticipated enrollment and financial difficulties, and efforts to strengthen the student affairs office.

Institutional Governance

How will the critical decisions about institutional response be made? What is the faculty's role in that process? American higher education has a strong tradition of faculty participation in decision-making. In practice, however, shared governance has always taken different forms.

First, faculty have consistently exercised influence by the constant inflow of faculty members into administrative positions: most key administrators were drawn from faculty ranks. Second, academic departments were the key link in shared governance, because they developed programs, hired faculty, and set standards of performance. Third, academic senates were formed to help advise administrators on institutionwide matters. During the 1960s, academic senates matured; in some cases their influence was substantial (for studies on these issues, see Baldridge, Curtis, Ecker, and Riley, 1978).

Threats to Shared Governance

Today, as enrollment and financial threats multiply, the governance situation has changed. In large state systems, faculty senates probably have lost some control over the institution because important decisions are increasingly made off-campus in the central system office or in the legislature. And on unionized campuses, the effectiveness of senates may be challenged to some extent by faculty unions as well as centralized administrations (see Baldridge and Kemerer, 1981).

Other factors suggest a weak role for faculty in the governance process. Roughly half of the presidents in our 1981 National Enrollment Survey agree with the statement, "The faculty here has only a perfunctory role in the preparation of the annual budget" (Table 12, Question 2). Considering that the budget process is a key decision-making event, such a large positive response to that question certainly testifies to weakness in the "shared governance" concept.

As retrenchment pushes hard decisions upward in the system, the influence of academic departments is substantially undermined. The right of academic departments to hire faculty, develop programs, and evaluate performance is often questioned. Departmental authority over program planning and staffing has been

Table 12: Presidents' Assessments of Faculty Involvement in Enrollment and Financial Concerns
(percentage of presidents who agree with statement)

Survey Question	Public Research Univ.	AASCU Inst.	Public 2-Year Coll.	Private Univ.	Private 4-Year Coll.	Private 2-Year Coll.	All Inst.
1. Faculty seem to understand this institution's financial concerns and problems.	73	66	68	69	75	67	70
2. Faculty here have only a perfunctory role in the preparation of the annual budget.	27	54	49	27	41	78	49
3. Over the last few years faculty here have had a greater role in the preparation of the annual budget.	64	62	57	64	65	44	59
4. Faculty seem to understand the basic underlying causes of the enrollment crisis forecast for the 1980s.	80	70	69	85	78	44	71
5. Faculty have been heavily involved in developing strategies to cope with enrollment concerns.	27	48	52	31	68	22	42

weakened because of tight budgets. Faculty unions are increasingly involved in setting the criteria for faculty performance. Budget-making authority is gradually moving upward, centralized in the hands of administrators, out of the reach of department faculty. The administrators have a clear rationale: times are lean and decisions must be centralized if waste and inefficiency are to be eliminated. The argument undoubtedly has some merit, but may be overstated.

There is another threat to shared governance. Although data are largely absent, we suspect that the inflow of faculty into administrative ranks has diminished. More and more we find that technocrats are running the shop—lawyers, financial experts, management information system specialists, and planning officers (see Kemerer and Baldridge, 1976, pp. 184-185). The tradition by which faculty members moved into administrative ranks and shaped institutional policy may be eroding. In some cases key state planning officers have never had actual responsibility in an educational organization; they have never been faculty members, never served as deans, and never been presidents of local campuses. But increasingly these technical specialists influence key decisions affecting academic policy.

Unionization is at least partly due to changes in academic governance. Ironically, unions have been an enormous stimulant to increased centralization. In large public systems, they are usually structured on a systemwide or statewide basis; they have a central headquarters much like the central administration of multicampus institutions. Highly centralized unions are a perfect counterpart to a highly centralized campus administration; and, in the long run, they cooperate with each other. (For an updated study on the impacts of collective bargaining see Baldridge and Kemerer, 1981.)

In short, it appears that shared governance may be an endangered species, especially in an era of retrenchment, financial uncertainty, and enrollment difficulties. Decision-making is moving higher into the administrative hierarchy and farther away from the point of action. Furthermore, at the statewide level decisions are increasingly lodged in legislative arenas, collective bargaining agencies, and the governor's office. Many presidents report that they feel they are middle managers rather than executives (see Baldridge and Kemerer 1981).

Ways to Strengthen the Governance Partnership

Faculty must confront the issues of institutional survival. Although presidents believe faculty recognize the enrollment problem, most do *not* see their faculties seriously involved in planning to meet the projected crisis (Table 12, Questions 4 and 5). That situation must be changed if faculty are to rally behind the changes that will be needed.

Second, faculty statesmen should lead the effort to revitalize university senates. Instead of being a forum for petty complaints, the senate should serve as the conscience of the college community. Instead of simply criticizing the administration, senates should also make strong statements against faculty provincialism and encourage faculty to look beyond their departments to institutionwide issues.

Third, faculty must become involved in union affairs. Although unions purport to represent everybody in the bargaining unit, in many situations unions are controlled by the narrow interests of disaffected and unhappy faculty members. To prevent this from happening, faculty who represent mainstream expertise and academic values must get involved in union affairs. The enrollment crisis—like it or not—will force retrenchment, and on unionized campuses senior faculty must work with the union as it struggles for fair decisions.

Case Study of Governance: SUNY-Potsdam

When confronted with severe strains and challenges, many campuses discover that the traditional governance mechanisms—academic departments, senates, and committees—are not adequate. Accustomed to dealing with growth, the traditional mechanisms become strained when the task is cutting back, redefining priorities, or preparing for enrollment declines. Consequently, many institutions find they must innovate, must devise new decision-making processes to help redefine priorities. The State University of New York College of Arts and Science at Potsdam provides an example of such innovation in governance as it prepares for an uncertain future. Because the changes at SUNY-Potsdam involve both governance and planning, we will review them in some depth.

Over the past several years, SUNY-Potsdam has favored a participatory approach to coping with serious financial problems and increased competition for a shrinking applicant pool. SUNY-Potsdam has involved representatives from all areas of the campus community in revising and articulating the college's mission. Campus planning is linked to budgetary allocations through a formal system of integrated planning and budgeting. Each department or school develops annual goals and objectives and these, in turn, determine enrollment targets.

Institutional Background

SUNY-Potsdam is a four-year arts and science college within the twenty-nine campus state-operated SUNY system. Like most of its sister four-year institutions, the college began as a teacher training institution, becoming a full-fledged multipurpose liberal arts college in 1962. Potsdam is located in a sparsely populated section of northern New York near the Canadian border.

SUNY-Potsdam has a current enrollment of more than 4,800 students, and has been successful in raising both the quality and number of its entering students. In 1981, the average SAT scores of its entering freshmen were 1020, 130 points above the national norm; the college exceeded its fall 1981 budgeted enrollment by 264 students.

Most of the college's clientele come from New York State (97 percent), with more than one-third coming from northern New York and the Albany area. Slightly over one-tenth come from the New York City area. Approximately one-half of the entering students leave the college before graduation, many going to other SUNY units to pursue programs not offered by Potsdam.

Potsdam's programs typify those of a small liberal arts and preprofessional college. One distinction is the Crane School of Music, nationally known for its preparation of music teachers who emphasize that their students have a strong performance orientation. Although the college has programs in graduate education and lifelong learning, the school's rural geographic location precludes the enrollment of substantial numbers of graduate adult and non-degree students.

SUNY-Potsdam does not have an enrollment problem at present. In the mid-1970s planners feared enrollment downturns. Consequently, the college moved aggressively to head off trouble—hiring an admissions consultant and building a very active and effective admissions office with five full-time recruiters, actions that produced a positive enrollment picture. Now, however, the college again fears it could have a serious enrollment problem in the 1980s, given the forecasted decline in numbers of New York State high school graduates, its chief source of students. Unlike metropolitan colleges and universities, SUNY-Potsdam will have more difficulty in attracting new clientele in meaningful numbers. Thus, to a large extent, the continuation of current enrollment patterns will depend on the college's ability to compete effectively with other institutions for students. The new governance and planning activities are a conscious effort to head off these anticipated enrollment difficulties. In addition, the campus already has *financial* difficulties owing to state cutbacks. From April 1980 to September 1982, the college was required to reduce its staff by thirty-one and did so without retrenchment of employed personnel. These reductions were part of a system-wide effort to reduce expenditures and were not necessarily related to the ability of individual campuses to enroll students. Further major cutbacks are likely at SUNY-Potsdam. In short, the college sees a need to prepare for both financial and enrollment uncertainties.

The Potsdam Approach to Planning and Governance

A new era of planning in SUNY began in 1976 when the master plan for the state university system called for each unit to develop missions to assess future directions. SUNY-Potsdam's former president, Thomas Barrington, established a committee to draft the institution's mission statement in two sections: an assessment of current service and data trends, and a narrative about future intentions. The mission statement was published in 1977.

In 1978, SUNY-Potsdam inaugurated a new president, James H. Young. One priority for the 1978-79 academic year was reviewing the college mission statement to ensure consensus about the document among the institution's constituencies. President Young set up a new collegewide committee cochaired by the vice president for academic affairs and the chairman of the Faculty Assembly.

The review committee studied the statement and agreed that it did reflect the college's mission. In response to the president's request to move to a Mission Action Plan (MAP), the committee identified eight key issues—enrollment, academic programs, nontraditional students and learning environments, liberal arts traditions, faculty and staff development, preparing students for an uncertain future, collection and management of information, and the allocation of resources. After extensive campuswide review of the draft, including a series of open hearings, the proposed action plan was approved by both the president and Faculty Assembly.

With the establishment of a multiyear MAP, an administrative structure was needed to continue the planning process and implement the plans. To create this, the president reorganized the Office of Institutional Research as the Office of Institutional Planning with broadened responsibility for planning, institutional research, and budgeting. This office serves as a catalyst for planning activities on the campus. In addition, the president established a broadly representative body to handle collegewide planning. This group was a carryover from the original committee that designed the mission statement. It was named the College Commission on Purposes and Priorities and has become instrumental in campus planning activities.

The commission annually reviews and revises the MAP. Based on this assessment, the commission develops recommendations for next year's institutionwide priorities. After consultation with the Faculty Assembly and the commission, the college president decides the institution's priorities, which in turn guide the development of school and departmental goals. Budget requests from departments and schools are judged by their relationship to college priorities. Through this process, the college expects to ensure the institution's continued strength and vitality.

Evaluating the Process: Some Positive Features

How successful is the planning process in ensuring institutional vitality? The planning process at SUNY-Potsdam is a good example of a bottom-up, participative approach to planning for an uncertain future. This approach contrasts with the top-down methods employed by many other colleges facing difficulties. Our case studies showed many instances of the opposite trend—

difficulty often provokes centralized, top-down planning. But the board of trustees at SUNY-Potsdam plays a very limited role in planning activities. Instead, there is great focus on "inductive" planning, with the specific college goals identified by the departments and schools within the context of the college's mission. Further, the link to budgetary decision-making gives the planning process an increased significance. In a time of shrinking resources, the institution must set budgetary priorities, and the MAP provides a direction for that decision-making.

Threats to the Potsdam Process

It is important to identify some problems that can arise with a process of this nature.

A Vague Mission Statement. Some department chairpersons are uncertain about the value of a MAP. One chairman noted cynically, "When I put my budget proposal together, I just look through MAP to find statements to justify it. MAP is so vague that it justifies anything—my being promoted or being retrenched!" Top administrators counter that this concern reflects inexperience, the difficulty of preparing a campuswide mission, and a healthy diversity of ideas. The challenge, top administrators argue, is to provide enough flexibility to encourage diversity but nevertheless to focus effort on mutually acceptable goals.

The Costs of Additional Clarity. Both administrators and faculty leaders expect to sharpen the focus of the MAP in the next several years. But here is a danger. If the MAP is used by administrators to justify program and personnel retrenchments, the faculty may cease to participate. Yet if the MAP remains too vague to have a shaping function, then the faculty may see the planning process as a waste of time.

The administration wants a judicious process by which reasonable decisions about the future can be made without involving the faculty directly in acrimonious decisions about resource allocation. President Young has repeatedly asserted that resource reallocation is solely a management responsibility. He does not want the MAP to be linked to cutbacks or retrenchment but, rather, to have planning be a positive, forward-looking process. Should retrenchment become necessary, a consultation process exists apart from the regular planning process. The president believes this approach will encourage faculty involvement in planning, at the same time keeping the burden of resource reallocation on the administration.

Limitations of the Mission Action Plan. More recently, information flow has improved as a result of having one administrative source—the Office of Institutional Planning—be responsible for data dissemination. However, faculty leaders argue that more data regarding institutional characteristics and the market environment need to be collected and shared.

The Role of the Faculty Union. The union concentrates on conditions of employment and salary. The college's Faculty Assembly, the major faculty governance body on campus, primarily addresses academic policy. The union plays a less active role in the planning process than the Faculty Assembly does. The union's continued support for the planning-budgeting process depends to a large extent on the union leadership. President Young has tried to balance the Faculty Assembly's concern for financial resources and the union's interest in personnel decisions, especially retrenchment. Whether this balance can be maintained remains to be seen, for finances, planning, and retrenchment are inevitably linked.

The Role of the Central Administration and the Division of the Budget. Although the SUNY Central Administration has not interfered extensively in campus internal affairs, the state centralized budgeting and accounting system has considerable influence over internal campus matters, especially those related to budget and personnel. Currently, President Young gets high marks for his effectiveness in political skills. But as one faculty member remarked, "We all suffer from 'Albany Anxiety'."

Summing Up: Lessons to be Learned

In a time of steadily diminishing resources, colleges will need a mechanism to establish priorities for programs and services so that effective budgetary decisions can be made. The SUNY-Potsdam approach represents one option that might be attractive to smaller institutions where faculty and staff play a major role in governance. Participatory planning does increase faculty and staff awareness, though it is often coupled with skepticism and a suspicion that the process is a paper chase and a management ploy. Nevertheless, the integration of institutional planning and departmental decision-making is a significant achievement.

The commitment and enthusiasm of top administrators (and trustees where they play a major role in institutional decision-making) is essential. During our interviews, some concern was expressed that President Young would leave just as the process was beginning to take hold, to be followed by a successor who might not support participatory planning. This could be a real problem, but if faculty commitment to the process is strong, a new president would probably continue to support it. As the chairman of the Commission on Purposes and Priorities observed to us, "As the faculty understand the process, they are more involved. Presidents come and go, but the system may get to the point where it will go on anyway." (This assertion will shortly be put to the test for President Young announced his departure in the summer of 1982 for a new position.)

Another key to success at SUNY-Potsdam is that the planning activities do not supplant the role of the Faculty Assembly but rather complement it. The Commission on Purposes and Priorities recommends goals and priorities to the president and Faculty Assembly. The assembly considers these proposals and makes its recommendations to the president, who is ultimately responsible for decision-making. Routing the priorities from the commission to the Faculty Assembly for their review is an important part of the planning process.

Staffing and Personnel Policies

Some of the most important strategic decisions involve staffing. The quality of key faculty and staff are probably the most important factors affecting an institution's ability to respond to an uncertain future. In many ways institutions have a golden opportunity to build high quality staffs because of the oversupply of Ph.D.'s in some fields.

Factors Eroding Faculty Quality

Since 1967 the Consumer Price Index has nearly tripled—it stood at 283 on April 15, 1982 (1967 = 100). In contrast, faculty salaries have lagged far behind the cost of living, averaging only about 244 on the index since 1967. Many state planners and trustees, while unhappy about this salary lag, nonetheless feel that the oversupply of Ph.D.'s, coupled with low salaries throughout higher education, gives faculty few options and makes for a "buyer's market." This is an entirely fallacious theory. The real question is not whether a bright young faculty member will leave a low paying job at UCLA and go to an equally low paying position at Yale. The real question is whether that person will leave UCLA to go to IBM. Furthermore, the oversupply is in low-demand areas (humanities, social sciences); there is a shortage in several such high-demand fields such as engineering, business, and computer science (see Solmon, Kent, Ochsner, and Hurwicz, 1981, Chapter 1).

A second quality-eroding factor is the effort of faculty unions to replace merit with seniority for pay increases and promotions. Where unions are strong, there is constant pressure to make seniority the key element in promotion, tenure, and protection against retrenchment. Administrations usually hold out for the concept of merit, for peer evaluation, and for rewarding talent—although some people charge these lofty sentiments actually cloak a desire to let administrators have the final decision. In the long run, however, the rash of grievances, lawsuits, and constant union pressure have caused many administrations to accept seniority rules. This trend seems to be accelerating, even in some nonunionized institutions.

The Debate over Part-Time Faculty

Consider this situation: an administration is unsure of the future, believes it has too many tenured faculty, and is frightened by a strong union that will fight tooth and nail if the institution ever tries to retrench faculty. Under these circumstances, it is only human that the administrators will look around for options that will keep them out of trouble. The common solution is to hire part-time faculty.

The evidence of a shift to part-time faculty is strong (see the complete discussion of this issue in Leslie, Kellams, and Gunne, 1982). In the last decade, the percentage of part-time staff among teaching faculty has increased rapidly. As Leslie, Kellams, and Gunne put it:

Part-timers evidently are quickly coming to play a much more important role than was believed even a short time ago. In any case, it appears safe to estimate that about 210,000-215,000 part-timers are currently at work and that they comprise about one-third of all faculty members at American colleges and universities. Variance among sectors is indeed great. Part-timers are most heavily used among major universities. Part-timers comprise more than one-half of all faculty in two-year colleges—in the fall of 1976, 55.8 percent . . . (1982, p. 18-19).

Our 1981 survey also lends strong support to this observation. Forty-four percent of college presidents agree that "We have made an effort to shift to part-time faculty in order to gain flexibility" (Table 13: Question 1). The two-year institutions lead the pack (65 percent of presidents agree). And that policy goal has been translated into action. Question 2 shows the strong move toward actually using part-time faculty—and two-year colleges again spearhead the drive.

The reasons for this shift are obvious. Part-time faculty do not have to be given tenure, they can be paid less than full-timer faculty, their benefits and insurance are not as great, and they can be released without serious repercussions when they are no longer needed. We can easily understand why administrators concerned about an uncertain future will turn to part-time faculty as a short-range solution.

What about the instructional practices of part-time faculty? A recent Center for the Study of Community Colleges report reveals that part-time faculty differed from the full-time faculty on most measures related to such practices. When compared to their full-time counterparts, part-time faculty were less experienced, held lower academic credentials, made fewer academic demands on students, were less involved in the campus community, and engaged in fewer professional development activities (see Friedlander, 1980, pp. 34-35).

Clearly there are many sides to this issue. Some women's groups may favor more part-time faculty positions to permit flexible work relations. Some technical fields may find that part-time faculty are the only—and best—way to staff their pro-

Table 13: Presidents' Assessments of Use and Performance of Part-Time Faculty
(percentage of presidents who agree with statement)

Survey Question	Public Research Univ.	AASCU Inst.	Public 2-Year Coll.	Private Univ.	Private 4-Year Coll.	Private 2-Year Coll.	All Inst.
1. We have made an effort to use more part-time faculty in order to gain staffing flexibility.	36	37	65	8	32	22	44
2. We have actually increased the number of part-time faculty as a proportion of the total faculty.	27	41	55	8	34	22	41
3. Part-time faculty do not perform as well as they should—even proportionately as well as their time commitments would indicate.	18	22	15	8	16	33	18

grams. But nagging doubts will continue about the impact on the careers and personal attitudes of the part-time faculty themselves, and on the quality of the educational program. What action needs to be taken on this important issue?

First, no institution should allow the number of part-time faculty to grow without serious planning. Every campus should constantly monitor its mix of part-time and full-time faculty.

Second, faculty unions should strive to upgrade the quality of life for part-time faculty. Unions should attempt to make part-time faculty just as costly as full-time faculty. The decision to hire part-time people should be made on educational and programmatic grounds rather than for budgetary reasons.

Finally, institutions must explore alternative styles for faculty employment. The current pattern is that full-time employment inevitably assumes tenure, that faculty organizations demand job security for full-time employees, and that the courts often favor the job rights of a dismissed full-time faculty member. It is no wonder that administrators with legitimate worries about maintaining flexibility will avoid the hassles of hiring full-time and instead opt for part-time faculty.

Institutions must explore more extensively the possibilities of full-time employment on fixed-term contracts that do not necessarily lead to tenure. A nontenure-track appointment with a fixed five-year contract, although not as desirable as a tenure-track position, may nevertheless be much better for an academic than a harried existence as a part-time faculty member. Between the open-ended flexibility of hiring part-time faculty and the inflexibility of hiring tenured faculty, the no-tenure, full-time approach may hold some promise as a reasonable middle ground. It preserves some degree of maneuverability, while capturing more dedication and full-time attention from the faculty. Hampshire College in Amherst, for example, uses a somewhat similar strategy. Private colleges will probably have more flexibility to explore such options, but public institutions should also attempt to generate new employment alternatives (see O'Toole, Van Alstyne, and Chait, 1980).

Other Policy Questions About Personnel

Our 1981 survey asked presidents about changes in personnel practices since 1975. Table 14 shows that the majority of institu-

Table 14: Presidents' Reports of Institutional Personnel Policies
(percentages)

Survey Questions	Public Research Univ.	AASCU Inst.	Public 2-Year Coll.	Private Univ.	Private 4-Year Coll.	Private 2-Year Coll.	All Inst.
1. Increased Activity Between 1975-1980							
a. Incentives for early retirement	27	24	24	58	14	0	19
b. Systematic efforts to evaluate faculty teaching competence	55	60	50	50	64	56	57
c. Systematic funded efforts to retain underutilized faculty for new or related fields or functions	9	30	29	9	26	11	25
2. Does Your Institution Have A Written Retrenchment Policy?							
Yes	36	60	59	8	19	0	38
No, but developing now	27	10	11	8	19	13	14
No, but anticipated by 1982	0	10	11	8	15	13	12
No, not anticipated	36	20	20	75	47	75	36

tions (57 percent) have increased efforts to evaluate teaching (Question I-b).

By contrast, surprisingly little attention has been given to incentives for early retirement (Question 1-a), retraining under-utilized faculty for new functions (Question 1-c), and retrench-ment plans (Question 2). These policies are often noted as key elements for planning a response to a possible enrollment decline. It is surprising that so little attention has been given to these key personnel policies.

Our case-study interviews suggest that administrators, union leaders, and state policy planners agree that carefully constructed retrenchment policies are essential. Although designing a retrench-ment policy is not easy, having such a document in advance is far superior to working without one or developing it when retrench-ment is required. There are sharp variations by type of institution: the public sector is clearly more prepared. Other data—not shown in the tables—suggest two critical facts. First, unionized campuses are far more likely to have a retrenchment policy. Perhaps one of the best contributions of collective bargaining has been to force the retrenchment issue to the front during negotiations. Second, private institutions anticipating the *worst* enrollment problems have done the *least* planning for retrenchment. This is a most discouraging observation, but it fits in rather clearly with the pattern of nonpreparation suggested in Table 14.

Some Reflections on Personnel Policies

As we look back over these personnel matters, several thoughts come to mind. First, local campus administrators cannot always have an impact even if they want to set different policies. For example, administrators at public institutions are caught in a web of state regulations, legislative fights over social priorities, and collective bargaining contracts that are often negotiated far from the campus. Certainly private sector administrators do not have a free hand, but their ability to maneuver is greater.

The point is that many public and private sector administra-tors *can* have influence. They can, for instance, have substantial control in many cases over institutional use of part-time faculty, innovations in full-time nontenure employment, development of retrenchment policies, and design of early retirement programs. Unfortunately, the record appears discouraging—much less effort has been spent on these contingency-planning issues than the changing circumstances require.

Strengthening the Student Affairs Office

The student affairs personnel on most campuses have a wide range of responsibilities in admissions, counseling, residence halls, registration, dean of student's office, campus union, and so forth. Unfortunately, some faculty and administrators view this as a no-man's land about which they know little and care less. As noted in chapter five, research on college impacts suggests the "student life" arena has a powerful influence on student development and growth.

Student services frequently suffer disproportionate reductions during major budget cuts. Faculty and administrators sometimes consider student life components to be frills that can be eliminated without harming the academic program. This may be a suicidal trend. Over the years many institutions have reduced the residential aspects of their campuses and become commuter institutions—colleges with large parking lots, few residence halls, and little opportunity for student involvement in campus life. For two decades institutions have given attention to expanding *access*, while at the same time reducing *impact*.

With the enrollment crisis looming on the horizon, student life components may determine the very survival of some institutions. Once students are enrolled, the quality of student life is a key element *keeping them* in college. The student services staff perform an enormously critical function for the institution, and they do not get the credit, pay, prestige, and respect they deserve.

Administrators and faculty members alike should take a strong interest in strengthening student affairs operations: budgets, services, and staffing. They should avoid the temptation to take money from these services to bolster faculty and administrative budgets. This overall piece of advice—strengthen student services—can be focused on two specific areas mentioned earlier in the book: effective student recruitment and retention.

Summary

This chapter discussed several major policy areas that must be confronted by any campus facing enrollment problems: (1) governance (2) personnel issues, and (3) links between student affairs personnel and faculty. While not directly related to student recruitment and retention, these policy areas provide opportunities for strategic decisions having a real impact on long-range institutional vitality and quality.

CHAPTER 8

The Concern for
Institutional Quality

There is widespread apprehension that for a variety of reasons higher education is cutting quality to sustain enrollments. This final chapter addresses several public policy questions about institutional quality:

- Is there really a decline in "quality," however one measures that elusive issue? We will look at programs, faculty, and students.

- Do institutions with enrollment difficulties dip lower in the student pool to recruit students, and do they cut quality in other ways? We will examine the data.

- How can institutions improve quality and also remain faithful to their espoused missions? Are there strategies that maintain quality despite declining enrollments? We will continue the discussion, begun in the previous chapter, of strategic decisions necessary for maintaining quality.

The Perception of Declining Quality: Myth or Reality?

All institutions and all good academics worship the Muse of Quality. Planning and policy decisions are made to maintain it. Three thousand colleges and universities claim they offer it. Accrediting associations attempt to assess it. Students, their families, government agencies, and the public-at-large are all concerned about it. That there is little consensus about what constitutes quality in higher education hardly matters. The range of contexts and concerns results in a variety of quality attributes that leave the meaning of the word elusive (Lawrence and Green, 1980). Nobody has satisfactorily defined quality, and we will not attempt to do so, except in a common-sense fashion.

The Debate

There is a major debate about quality in American higher education. Some evidence suggests significant decline; still other evidence implies improvements.

The symptoms of declining quality are well known: dropping test scores, fewer job options for college graduates, displacements in the academic labor market, and declining literacy among college students. While the public may sometimes appear tolerant of collegiate athletic scandals, there is deep-seated concern about academic scandal—faked research results, unearned course credits, and questionable degrees. Furthermore, the debate over student and faculty affirmative action policies and meritocratic selection practices—a debate best symbolized by the 1978 *Bakke* case—contributes to public and legislative concerns about *quality* as well as *equality* in postsecondary education. Finally, the shortcomings of some radical educational reforms from the 1960s and 1970s have affected the discussion about quality. There is a growing feeling in academe that excellence and innovation, at least as manifested in the 1960s and 1970s, may not be as compatible as many reformers had hoped (Grant and Riesman, 1978; Levine, 1981).

Yet signs also abound that quality has improved in the past two decades. More and different kinds of students now have access to postsecondary education. More faculty have earned doctoral degrees. Real dollar support for postsecondary education continues to grow.

Public Policy Issues

Over the years, the Gallop Poll has documented erosion of public confidence in higher education. Between 1966 and 1979 the percentage of Americans who expressed confidence in higher education dropped from 61 percent to 32 percent. Many educators, politicians, and citizens question the *qualitative* aspects of the academic community's dramatic postwar growth. Thomas Stauffer, formerly of the American Council on Education, observes that the quality issue is high on the neoconservative agenda for higher education, "notably the quality of education received, of research and service, of program and personnel evaluation, and institutional productivity, academic freedom, and governmental influence" (1981, p. 66).

In a similar vein, Chester Finn has discussed the reemerging concern with quality in American education in both the *Wall Street Journal* and in *Change* (Finn, 1981a; 1981b). He writes that "quality is almost certainly going to be the foremost educational concern of the 1980's much as equity was the premier issue of the 1960's and 70's" (Finn, 1981b, p. 21).

Growing public and governmental concern about quality has led to severe criticism of accreditation—the oldest and most widely recognized indication of quality in higher education. Accreditation is the academic community's attempt at self-regulation, but some observers charge that accreditation often fails to distinguish program and institutional quality. Quality exists on a continuum, but accreditation operates on a "pass-fail" system. Accreditation may be further undermined by recent research suggesting that regional associations' accrediting criteria "assume common benchmarks exist for assessing institutional quality" (Troutt, 1979, p. 201). Other research suggests that on-site accreditation team members rank quality behind other objectives as a goal of accreditation reviews (Silvers, 1982, Table 2). Although government agencies have tried not to undermine the accreditation/self-regulation process, federal and state agencies have expressed concern about accreditation as a vehicle for ensuring institutional quality. Indeed, some agencies have notified regional accreditation associations that they intend to play a more active role in the accreditation process.

Research Perspectives on the Issue of Quality

Has quality really declined? The results of the 1981 National Enrollment Survey, coupled with other research, indicate that there has been improvement in some areas and decline in others.

Institutional and Program Quality

Although college presidents are concerned about quality, the 1981 National Enrollment Survey suggests that their concerns are global (problems affecting all of higher education) rather than local (issues affecting my campus).

Presidents generally report qualitative improvements on their campuses. Look at Table 15. It reveals several facts:

• Very few presidents (6 percent) feel the reputation of their campus has declined since 1975 (Question 1).

• A large majority (71 percent) feel the faculty quality is up (Question 2).

• A large majority (76 percent) think academic programs have improved (Question 3).

These results are fairly consistent across different institutional types, except for public community colleges, whose presidents are not quite as optimistic as other presidents. Compared to the presidents of other institutions, AASCU presidents are slightly less likely to report qualitative improvement among faculty but slightly more likely to report improved academic programs. Similar trends have been reported by John Minter and Howard Bowen on a smaller sample of institutions (Minter and Bowen, 1982).

There are many reasons presidents report qualitative improvements during the last half of the 1970s. First, the Ph.D. surplus resulted in an increase in the proportion of faculty who have a doctorate. Moreover, the decline of the academic labor market over the last ten years has no doubt contributed to an "academic trickle-down" whereby graduates of prestigious doctoral programs are now found in less prominent institutions. Moreover, despite high inflation during the 1970s, the actual dollar value of financial resources for most postsecondary institutions stayed even with or slightly ahead of the Consumer Price Index during the past decade (National Center for Educational Statistics, 1981, pp. 172-173).

Program reviews, initiated by campus or state authorities, may have contributed to improvement in academic programs, at least in public institutions. Our survey data reveal that public institution presidents feel that their campuses' abilities to mount

Table 15: Presidential Perspectives on Institutional Quality
(percentage of presidents who strongly agree or agree)

Survey Question	Public Research Univ.	AASCU Inst.	Public 2-Year Coll.	Private Univ.	Private 4-Year Coll.	Private 2-Year Coll.	All Inst.
1. Academic reputation of this institution has declined since 1975	0	4	5	0	7	11	6
2. Quality of faculty has improved since 1975	75	72	61	85	76	78	71
3. Quality of academic programs has improved since 1975	73	84	66	85	80	89	76

new degree programs have been constrained by state program review (data not shown).

In addition, the difficulties in the academic labor market and the academic community's financial problems during the 1970s permitted institutions to expand faculty evaluation practices. Table 16 shows that presidents of four-year colleges and universities report increased institutional efforts to evaluate faculty teaching performance, as well as rising standards for faculty salary, promotion, and tenure decisions. By contrast, although community college presidents report more efforts to evaluate teaching performance, a lesser proportion report rising standards in other areas. All these issues are covered in Table 16, which deserves close examination.

Student Quality: Survey Perceptions

The biggest argument in the quality debate concerns students. Here is the critics' charge: "Is it not true that in spite of better faculty, greater access, and more resources students are less well prepared at entry, drop out more frequently, and learn less?" We cannot completely refute all these charges, but at least we can marshal some data.

First, presidents do report that student preparation for college has declined. (See Table 17, Question 2). Over half (53 percent) agree that "the quality of high school preparation among our students has declined in the past five years." Roughly one-third disagree with this assessment. But note the interesting paradox in Table 17. Although most presidents see a decline in the preparation of entering students, most also report an increase in student quality! Interestingly, only 15 percent report that the quality of students has declined since 1975, whereas 31 percent report no change in student quality and 54 percent say that student quality has improved. Private research universities appear to have "won" the student recruitment competition of the mid-1970s; presidents of these institutions are much more likely to report both that student quality has improved and that student preparation has not declined.

Although most college presidents believe that student quality has improved, admissions directors report very little change in their freshman students between 1975 and 1980. Only 12 percent of admissions directors report an increase in the freshman high

Table 16: Presidents Reporting Increases in Personnel Programs, 1975-1980
(percentages)

Survey Question	Public Research Univ.	AASCU Inst.	Public 2-Year Coll.	Private Univ.	Private 4-Year Coll.	Private 2-Year Coll.	All Inst.
1. Systematic efforts to evaluate faculty teaching competence	55	60	50	50	64	56	57
2. Rigor of standards for faculty salary decisions	54	43	18	67	43	33	34
3. Rigor of standards for faculty promotion	81	62	10	75	58	44	42
4. Rigor of faculty tenure standards	81	58	10	75	61	57	42

Table 17: Presidential Perceptions of Student Quality
(percentage of presidents who strongly agree or agree)

Survey Question	Public Research Univ.	AASCU Inst.	Public 2-Year Coll.	Private Univ.	Private 4-Year Coll.	Private 2-Year Coll.	All Inst.
1. Quality of students has improved since 1975	36	56	51	77	53	66	54
2. There has been decline in student preparation for college	64	51	45	18	59	66	53

school rank between 1975 and 1980, 81 percent report no change, and 7 percent report a decline (Table 18).

These figures differ markedly from the presidential perceptions reported in Table 17, where over half the presidents report that student quality has improved. The disparity in the perceptions of presidents and admissions directors is greatest in AASCU institutions and private universities. Nearly 56 percent of AASCU presidents report improved student quality, but over 80 percent of AASCU admissions officers report no change in the freshmen profile. Similarly, over 75 percent of private university presidents perceived improvements in student quality during the late 1970s, but only 14 percent of the admissions directors in these institutions report any improvement. Why the stark differences—presidents seeing improved student quality, admissions directors seeing stability? And who is right? Of course rightness depends on subtle value judgments, but we suspect admissions directors are probably closer to the truth.

Student Quality: SAT Scores

What about the widely discussed decline in test scores of entering students over the past decade? Nationwide. the mean composite (verbal plus math) score on the SAT declined by 36 points or 3.9 percent between 1973 and 1980 (College Board, 1981). Yet there have been substantial differences in SAT score decline of students by institutional type.

The SAT decline has been greatest for students entering public four-year colleges; private universities have actually become slightly more selective. Between 1973 and 1980, the average SAT scores of entering freshman dropped 1.8 percent for private universities, 3.9 percent for private four-year colleges, 4.8 percent for public universities, and 5.4 percent for public four-year colleges. In this last group—largely AASCU institutions—the decline in freshman scores was roughly 40 percent more than the overall SAT decline in the applicant pool—3.9 percent (Henson, forthcoming).

Some might argue that the decline at public institutions reflects a growing number of minority and adult students in the college population. These students tend to score lower than the traditional 18-22 year-old cohort. However, College Board officials

**Table 18: Changes in the High School Rank of Entering
Freshman Class, by Institutional Type, 1975-1980**
(percentage of admissions directors reporting change)

Type of Institution	Increased (123)*	Same (2012)*	Decreased (295)*
All Institutions	12	81	7
Public Institutions			
Research Universities	0	100	0
AASCU Members	3	84	13
Two-Year Colleges	4	92	4
Private Institutions			
Universities	14	86	0
Four-Year Colleges	6	75	19
Two-Year Colleges	20	70	10

*Number of directors reporting.

report that the proportion of minority and older students taking the SAT has stablized since 1970.

A more likely explanation is that state colleges and universities have become more conscious of their mission to provide access than have other types of institutions. At the same time, many public four-year colleges have found their stronger students enticed away by aggressive recruiting from public and private universities, which could offer more attractive financial-aid packages in the 1970s. As a result, SAT scores declined more rapidly at state colleges and universities than at other types of institutions. Recent cutbacks in financial aid opportunities, however, are likely to reverse the trend in the future as students seek out the less expensive institutions.

Student Quality: Admissions Selectivity and Enrollment Levels

Table 19 shows admissions directors' responses to several questions concerning high school rank and enrollment levels between 1975 and 1980. This table is a cross-tabulation: it does not show cause and effect relationships. Look at Question 1. Institutions experiencing declines in high school rank of entering freshman split evenly between increases and decreases in numbers of applications. By contrast, 84 percent of institutions reporting increases in high school rank also reported increases in applications, and only 6 percent reported declines.

This same pattern of high correlation between increases in numbers of student acceptances and subsequent enrollments and increases in the high school rank of the freshman class is evident in Questions 2-4 of Table 19. The data thus suggest that raising selectivity standards does not automatically result in an enrollment decrease. However, neither does *lowering* selectivity standards automatically produce the expected increase in numbers of students.

Obviously, if all campuses were to raise selectivity standards, there would not be enough students to go around. Moreover, a concern for "quality" cannot be assigned only to those institutions that enroll the strongest students. An argument can be made that many open-access institutions actually provide greater educational benefits to their students than do those that, as one commentator noted, "preselect winners."

Table 19: Changes in Applications, Enrollments, and Selectivity among Four-Year Colleges and Universities, 1975-1980

(percentage of admissions directors who responded)

Survey Question	High School Rank of Freshman Class		
	Declined (N=57)	Same (N=935)	Improved (N=206)
1. Number of Applications			
Decreased	44	11	6
No Change (±3%)	10	23	10
Increased	46	66	84
Total	100	100	100
2. Number of Admitted Freshmen			
Decreased	20	12	9
No Change (±3%)	14	28	16
Increased	66	60	75
Total	100	100	100
3. Number of Full-Time Freshmen			
Decreased	40	13	9
No Change (±3%)	40	31	16
Increased	20	56	75
Total	100	100	100
4. Total Enrollment			
Decreased	29	12	11
No Change (±3%)	48	24	12
Increased	11	65	77
Total	100	100	100

We do not wish to take sides in this debate. All we wish to do is point out that traditional assumptions about the relationship between student selectivity standards and enrollment levels are highly suspect.

Alfred University: A Decision to Pursue Quality

It is easy enough to discuss the abstract characteristics of quality. It is also easy to urge faculty and administrators to work to maintain institutional quality and academic integrity. But what happens when an institution makes a strategic decision to pursue quality—to maintain academic standards and admissions requirements even if enrollments drop and revenues decline? What are the consequences of strategic decision to pursue quality? J. Victor Baldridge in *Power and Conflict in the University* shows how New York University made such a bold step in the late 1960s and early 1970s—and the gamble paid off (Baldridge, 1971). In our current case studies we found other instances of such aggressive policies. SUNY-Potsdam, for example, set a five-year goal of raising combined SAT scores of entering students 15 points per year and high school averages one point per year. Between 1979 and 1982, SAT scores rose from 1,005 to 1,048, while average high school grades increased from 85.7 to 87.9. During the same period, the number of applications and enrollees increased. In this section, we look at Alfred University and analyze yet another institution's route to quality.

In 1975, Alfred University, a private university located in southwestern New York, made a strategic decision to increase admissions standards, raise academic requirements, and improve academic programs. Faculty and administrators knew that this was a gamble—particularly given the extensive competition for college students among private colleges in New York and other eastern states, coupled with the severe enrollment decline forecast for the region. Could the college promote quality, increase admissions requirements, and recruit enough students to survive? Did the university have the faculty resources to work with brighter students? How would the university survive a period of retrenchment if enrollments fell short of goals? These and other questions were discussed by Alfred's faculty and administrators prior to the policy change. Ultimately, the university community decided that the quality of students and academic programs was an essential component of future enrollment management efforts.

Context of the Decision

Prior to the late 1960s, Alfred University enjoyed a good reputation for its academic programs and personalized student service. The university was not concerned with size but with maintaining its traditional academic offerings to qualified students. However, in 1967, Alfred, like a number of other institutions, made a decision to increase enrollments. For the next seven to eight years the university accepted academically "weaker" students as it concentrated on growth. The university's reputation changed. Alfred was now alleged to be an "easy" school—easy to get in, easy to stay in.

The consequences of the decision to increase enrollments did not sit well with many faculty and administrators. They were not pleased with the university's eroding reputation and declining standards. The arrival of a new president in 1974 marked a turning point. Alfred's new president, Richard Rose, was committed to the concept of quality. Rose was also responsive to faculty concerns for academic standards and was willing to study underlying problems at Alfred. The university knew that although enrollments had increased during the late 1960s and early 1970s, the selectivity of the students had declined and top prospective students were choosing New York's public colleges over Alfred. The university had to assess its situation and make a strategic decision about growth, enrollment, and quality that would have important short- and long-term consequences.

The Strategic Decision: Promoting Quality

Alfred University's approach to enrollment management focused on one target: the concept of quality in the light of its projected impact on future enrollment. In 1974 the major concern of the new administration and the faculty was the quality of students being attracted to Alfred. At that time, the university admitted 90 percent of its applicants. Total university enrollment figures had risen to over 2,000 students. However, both administrators and faculty realized that a long-range view of enrollment had to address quality issues if the university were to remain viable.

Following a period of intensive assessment and discussion, administrative officers and faculty concluded that student and academic program quality were essential to the institution's future. Moreover, both groups, working together, concluded that Alfred did have the faculty resources needed for placing major emphasis on student and academic program quality.

These were not easy decisions for Alfred. Faculty and administrators recognized a number of short-term problems. Efforts to raise admissions standards might result in an initial decline in freshman applications and enrollments. House-cleaning of academic programs would probably require some faculty retrenchment. However, these issues were viewed as short-term problems—necessary but instrumental consequences of pursuing the ultimate goal to improve academic programs, raise admissions standards, and increase enrollments. Faculty, generally threatened by any talk of retrenchment, nonetheless supported the proposed changes. Many saw it as returning to the traditional characteristics that had been the hallmark of the university in an earlier period.

Implementation: Pursuing Quality

Alfred's admissions staff was given primary responsibility for developing a strategy to improve standards and maintain enrollments, seemingly an impossible task. A new academic scholarship program, announced at a 1974 dinner for high school counselors, was Alfred's first strategic move to pursue top-quality students. All qualified applicants could receive these new academic, no-need scholarships. Publications were revised to stress the quality of Alfred's academic programs, the highly personal nature of the educational experience, and the quality of student service programs. The university emphasized its liberal arts programs, and stressed the career and graduate school experiences of its graduates.

Alfred's efforts to improve quality were not limited to admissions requirements and recruitment practices. When faculty and administrators made the decision to pursue quality, they also identified the characteristics of current programs that were most important. Program diversity and personalized services were identified as distinguishing features of the university—

features that were to be maintained and enhanced. Consequently, the university stresses student-faculty interaction. Faculty evaluation criteria stress teaching performance and academic advising. That faculty are to meet with their advisees at least once every three weeks became official university policy.

These changes were not initiated without some problems. The change in admissions standards led to enrollment declines. Some junior faculty were not retained. Eighteen faculty were denied tenure because of the university's retrenchment program between 1975 and 1980. Some tenured faculty were also retrenched. However, the retrenchment plan developed by a committee of department heads focused on improving quality without cutting programs deemed essential to the institution's mission. Consequently, the eventual cutbacks were limited largely to language and performing arts programs, which had traditionally been service areas for other degree programs.

Quality at Alfred: An Assessment

In short, enrollment management at Alfred University focuses on academically strong students and rigorous academic programs. Strategies used to attain these goals include a scholarship program to attract top students, personalized student services, and a concentrated effort on building diversity in the academic program.

Has it worked? Has Alfred University been able to increase standards, improve programs, and also maintain enrollments? The evidence suggests that Alfred University has done so. Although these goals were not accomplished without some serious short-term problems, Alfred's strategic decision to pursue quality must be judged a success so far.

Table 20 provides an academic enrollment profile for Alfred University from 1971-1981. In sum, the data reveal that since fall 1975—the turning point at which Alfred decided not to pursue growth but to pursue quality—the academic profile of entering students has improved, enrollment has stabilized, and retention has increased.

We want to highlight the improvement in student retention (Table 20). Although freshman retention has improved slightly, there has been a very significant change in the four-year retention rate, i.e., the proportion of entering freshmen who graduate in

Table 20: Academic and Enrollment Profile for Alfred University, 1971-1981

Category	1971	1972	1973	1974	1975	1976	1977	1978	1979	1980	1981
Percentage of Freshman in Top Fifth of High School Graduating Class	31%	28%	24%	23%	31%	31%	35%	40%	42%	48%	54%
SAT Scores											
Verbal Mean	528	499	497	460	460	462	480	472	475	476	480
Math Mean	566	543	533	500	510	527	536	519	528	542	533
Enrollment											
Freshman	594	570	508	503	472	402	438	377	494	480	483
Total Undergraduate	2170	2244	2219	2077	2021	1872	1852	1819	1845	1929	2010
Retention											
Freshman (returning for sophomore year)	79%	79%	73%	85%	79%	85%	86%	N/A	86%	85%	N/A
Four-Year (graduating within four years).	N/A	63%	N/A	61%	56%	57%	51%	55%	61%	65%	65%

four years. Because the four-year rate has improved, Alfred can continue to be selective about its students. Improved retention means that the college does not need six hundred freshmen each year to maintain its total enrollment of roughly 2,000. Improved retention has contributed to growing enrollments despite increasing competition for new students and the beginnings of the demographically stimulated enrollment crisis. In short, the cycle worked: improved selectivity equalled better retention equalled less need for new enrollees.

Stable enrollments have also led to the rebuilding of academic programs that experienced retrenchment during the period Alfred's faculty refer to as the "Dark Ages." The university recently added a new Division of Industrial Engineering, complementing its other recognized engineering programs. New programs are being developed in computer science and gerontology. Language and performing arts programs that were cut back some years ago are also being modestly expanded.

Alfred University is a good case study of an institution's strategic decision to pursue student and program quality. Faculty and administrators are convinced that the decision to focus on quality was the right decision, one that has enhanced institutional vitality, academic quality, and future enrollments. Recognizing that its liberal arts tradition and rural geographic location severely restricted the university's ability to attract new clientele, Alfred fell back on its tradition of rigorous programs and personalized services—and then made a series of critical decisions to enhance both. Although the university experienced some short-term problems, its long-term enrollment and financial prospects appear good.

Strategies for Maintaining Quality

Certainly the demographic events and financial problems forecast for the 1980s threaten the integrity of the academic enterprise. What happens to quality during a prolonged period of enrollment decline and financial difficulty? What can faculty and administrators do to maintain quality? And how should these efforts be linked to the institutional mission?

In the previous two chapters we discussed several strategic decisions related to institutional vitality and strength. In the remainder of this chapter we identify three additional decision areas that can have a profound impact on institutional and program quality.

Academic Requirements

It is clear that a decade of curricular experimentation and drift has had a negative impact on student preparation for college. Many colleges—particularly flagship universities and major private institutions—reduced admissions requirements for applicants and course requirements for undergraduates. Reduced admissions requirements "trickled down" into the college preparatory curriculum in the high schools. College and high school students opted for the obvious expedient route and took fewer courses in such areas as English, foreign language, science, and mathematics.

Yet institutions do have considerable control over the academic programs of their undergraduates and the academic preparation of their applicants. A number of public and private institutions have recently revised their undergraduate programs and raised degree requirements. Several major public institutions recently raised admissions standards (Western Interstate Commission, 1982). In some instances, public institutions have raised the minimum grade average required for admission. Other institutions have raised the academic course requirements for admission. In California and New Mexico, university officials have moved to increase the academic preparation of prospective students by increasing the number and specifying the kinds of college preparatory courses required for admission.

The experience of the past decade suggests that students and secondary schools do respond to academic incentives and entrance requirements established by colleges and universities. In this context, quality has a "trickle-down" component: if colleges increase course prerequisites for admission, these changes do affect secondary schools and high school students. We encourage all institutions to review current academic requirements for degree programs and for admission. We suspect that institutions can increase prerequisites without harming enrollments; indeed, doing so may help sustain and perhaps increase enrollments.

Increased entry requirements would certainly improve academic preparation and would contribute to the overall quality of both secondary and postsecondary education..

We recognize, however, that many institutions have little control over this issue. At some public institutions, for example, admissions criteria are often established by external bodies such as regents or trustees, or even a state legislature. A policy of open admissions certainly limits the option to raise entrance requirements. The pursuit of quality at open institutions must begin once students enroll. Remedial courses in verbal and mathematical skills, required core programs, and comprehensive examinations for graduation represent options for increasing the impact of these campuses on student quality. Experience suggests that students recognize quality when they see it and may well be attracted rather than repelled by academically challenging programs.

Academic Rigor

Accompanying the lowering of academic requirements has been a major decline in standards for student academic performance, both in high schools and in colleges and universities. For example, the proportion of college freshmen who were A or A- students in high school rose from 12 percent in 1966 to 21 percent in 1982; C students dropped from 32 percent to 19 percent of the freshman class during the same period (Astin, King, and Richardson, 1982). In colleges and universities, the proportion of A students more than doubled between 1969 and 1976, from 7 to 19 percent, while the proportion of C students declined from 40 to 25 percent (Carnegie Council, 1979). Yet, few would cite rising grade averages as evidence that students know more or perform better than their counterparts of a decade ago, particularly given the decline of student scores on standardized tests and the growing concern about student competencies in composition, mathematics, and science.

A number of institutions have recently initiated plus-minus grading programs to address the needs for academic rigor and increased standards for academic performance.

Faculty, academic departments, and academic policy-makers should try to instill rigor into academic programs. Like academic requirements, academic rigor is a quality variable that is affected by institutional policies and procedures.

What does it mean to increase academic rigor and standards? We suggest that rigor is reflected in course objectives and program goals that are intellectually challenging; rigor is not synonymous with unreasonable demands on students. Rigor can be linked to clear learning objectives. Rigor does mean that students know what is required for an A and how they can become competent in the subject matter. Rigor involves more than adding increments to an inflated grading system.

Cohesive efforts to instill rigor into the college curriculum will contribute to institutional and program quality. Several authors suggest that when students are challenged by the college curriculum they invest more time and effort into learning activities (Astin, 1971, 1977).

Program Review

Rising concern for quality is the current manifestation of efforts in postsecondary education that began in the 1970s. The accountability movement has emphasized quality, educational effectiveness, and resource efficiency. Accountability focuses on results and "aims squarely at what comes out of an educational system rather than what goes into it" (Mortimer, 1972, p. 6). Similarily, state program review, an outgrowth of the accountability movement, has evolved from appraising new program proposals to assessing existing programs. Program review generally encompasses both qualitative and financial concerns and has been successful at using a range of measures to assess institutional quality (Green 1981).

Yet program review, by name, is not a new activity in higher education. Departments, institutions, accrediting associations, and state agencies have always conducted periodic reviews and assessments of academic programs. In recent years, however, the force behind program review has moved off-campus: program review now appears to be the responsibility of a state agency rather than a local campus option.

Program review is not a very popular activity, in part because it is often directed by external agencies. Critics of program review cite several problems. First, because program review is often linked to termination, the process has become increasingly political, pitting departmental leaders against campus and/or system office administrators. Second, program review is often an expensive, lengthy process that yields little change. Third, the evaluation criteria are often very politicized. Some efforts emphasize quality while others focus on the centrality of the program to the institution's mission. In many cases, the quality criteria employed are often broader than traditional quality notions.

Financial problems and retrenchment will force many campuses to reassess program priorities. Yet administrators and faculty generally are unwilling to establish the criteria for retrenchment and program termination decisions. All too often administrators pass budget cuts down to departments in the form of across-the-board cuts; they avoid targeting cuts at specific program areas. Even when faculty reductions are not involved, it is difficult for professors to accept the idea that new programs and qualitative improvements can be introduced only at the expense of other programs. Unfortunately, in many institutions it is no longer a matter of cutting low-quality, marginal programs, but programs that are viewed as laudable and needed but deemed too expensive to maintain.

Institutions should use program review as a vehicle for quality enhancement. All too often organizational policy-making is an incremental process, driven by variables such as the budget and institutional revenues. Academic program review initiated by the institution is a viable method of assessing and improving program and campus quality.

Summary

This chapter has reviewed much of the discussion about the data on quality in American higher education. A number of indicators suggest that certain programmatic aspects affecting quality have improved in recent years. However, other indicators, such as student test scores and grade inflation, point to a decrease in quality and student preparation. Our survey data indicate that many institutions experiencing enrollment declines have also experienced a decline in the academic quality of admitted students.

We believe that quality is an essential component of the academic enterprise. Consequently, we have identified several strategic decisions that have a direct impact on program and institutional quality. Institutions can affect and improve the level of academic requirements and academic rigor. They should review academic programs to identify areas for improvement. Institutions do have tremendous control over many factors that contribute to program quality and institutional integrity. We urge faculty and administrators to make the strategic decisions that will, over the long term, have positive consequences for quality in post-secondary education.

We began in chapter one by acknowledging that we, like other commentators, do not really know what the future of higher education is. Current demographic and financial realities suggest a decline in enrollment at many institutions through this decade. This being the case, we have proposed in this book a number of direct and indirect strategies administrators and faculty can use to manage enrollments effectively. All are of the day-to-day, middle-range type. We have avoided the long-range grand design because the world of higher education management doesn't operate that way. Likewise, we have avoided the lure of quick-fix solutions like those so often portrayed in marketing literature.

Effective enrollment management begins at home with concerned and knowledgeable administrators and faculty who realize that they possess the capacity to respond creatively to environmental pressures in the interest of long-term institutional health. We hope that some of the insights and strategies discussed in this book will help in that endeavor.

APPENDIX A
Sample Reporting Forms

Sample Reporting Form I

Freshmen Admissions Flow

Category	1975	1976	1977	1978	1979	1980	1981	1982**
Applicants								
Admitted								
% Admitted								
Enrolled								
Yield*								

Transfer Admissions Flow

Category	1975	1976	1977	1978	1979	1980	1981	1982*
Applicants								
Admitted								
% Admitted								
Enrolled								
Yield*								

Graduate Admissions Flow

Category	1975	1976	1977	1978	1979	1980	1981	1982*
Applicants								
Admitted								
% Admitted								
Enrolled								
Yield*								

* (The "yield" is the proportion of admitted students who choose to enroll in the fall of that year.)
**This information should be obtained on a month-by-month basis for the current year and compared with the same time period the previous year. Doing so will allow campus administrators to change recruiting strategy and shift resources to meet changing conditions.

Sample Reporting Form II

Freshman (or Transfer, Graduate) Applications by Program

Program	Application Number	Percent of Total	Mean SAT of Applicants	Number Admitted	Number Enrolled	Mean SAT of Enrolled	%Yield* 1980	%Yield* 1981
Undeclared								
Arts and Science								
Art								
Biochemistry								
Biology								
Chemistry								
Computer Science								
Economics								
English								
French								
—etc—								
College of Business								
Accounting								
Business Education								
Finance								
Marketing								
Real Estate								
Secretarial Admin.								
—etc—								
College of Education								
Elementary								
—etc—								
Total								

*The "yield" is the proportion of admitted students who choose to enroll.

Sample Reporting Form III

Counselors and Individual School Visits

County	High School	No. Seen	Reception	Counselor	Applications	Acceptances
Acme	Crosby	0	Excellent	John Jones	6	0
	Pioneer	14	Fair	John Jones	2	1
	Thumper	22	Excellent	John Jones	4	2
	Watertown	8	Good	Phil Smith	10	8
	Weedsport	30	Excellent	Phil Smith	20	15
etc.	etc.	etc.	etc.	etc.	etc.	etc.

Sample Reporting Form IV

Annual Undergraduate Attrition

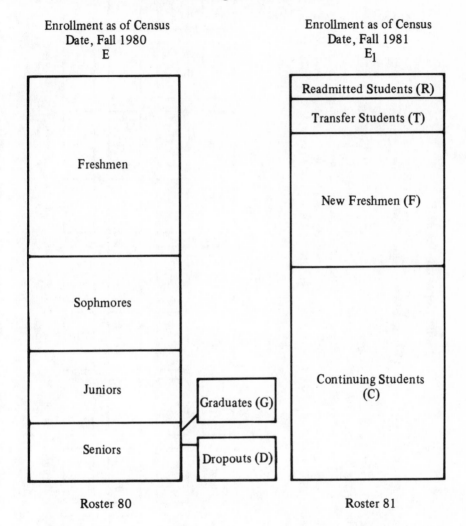

Enrollment as of Census
Date, Fall 1980
E

Freshmen

Sophmores

Juniors

Graduates (G)

Seniors

Dropouts (D)

Roster 80

Enrollment as of Census
Date, Fall 1981
E_1

Readmitted Students (R)

Transfer Students (T)

New Freshmen (F)

Continuing Students
(C)

Roster 81

Note: Based on the number of students enrolled during the previous year (E), you then subtract the number of new freshmen (F), new and previously admitted transfer students (T), readmitted students (R), continuing students (C), and graduates (G) to determine the number of drop-outs over the course of the year. To determine number of dropouts:

1) $C = E_1 - R - T - F$

2) Potential C (PC) = $E - G$

3) Dropouts = $PC - C$

Sample Reporting Form V

Cohort Flow – Data Sheet

Note: Beginning in Block A1, enter the number of new freshmen enrolled in any one particular year. In Block A2 enter the number of entering freshmen who returned the following fall as sophomores. Additionally, because some students will transfer into the college as sophomores, enter the number of second year transfer students into Block B2. Following the chart through helps to track the number of continuing and new transfer students and to monitor the number of students in a particular class who graduate or who require additional time beyond four years to complete their degrees.

	Entering Freshmen Transfer	Entering Sophomore Transfer	Entering Junior Transfer	Entering Senior Transfer	Graduates Year IV	Continuing Students Year IV	Graduates Year V	Continuing Students V	Graduates Year VI	Continuing Students	Graduates Year VI	Total Graduates
				D4	GD1	D5	GD2	D6	GD3	GD		GD
			C3	C4	GC1	C5	GC2	C6	GC3	GC		GC
		B2	B3	B4	GB1	B5	GB2	B6	GB3	GB		GB
	A1	A2	A3	A4	GA1	A5	GA2	A6	GA3	GA		GA
	Year I	Year II	Year III	Graduates Year IV	Continuing Students Year IV	Graduates Year V	Continuing Students V	Graduates Year VI			Total Graduates	

APPENDIX B

Sources for Further Reading

A few of the more useful sources on topics related to enrollment management are described in this appendix. A more detailed review of the literature is reflected in our research monograph, *Enrollments in the Eighties: Crisis, Myths, and Realities,* (1982).

Carnegie Council on Policy Studies in Higher Education. *Three Thousand Futures: The Next Twenty Years for Higher Education.* San Francisco: Jossey-Bass, 1980.

The final volume of the Carnegie Council books is actually two reports. The first half of the book provides an overview of such issues as demographic shifts and enrollment decline, shifting patterns of financial support for higher education, and the changing labor market for college graduates. The second portion of the volume consists of resource documents that present data on such issues as institutional finances, enrollment projections, educational opportunity, and faculty development, among others. The volume emphasizes enrollment issues in the 1980s, and outlines many of the critical factors which will affect institutional vitality in the 1980s and 1990s.

College Entrance Examination Board. *Marketing College Admissions: A Broadening of Perspectives.* New York: College Board, 1980.

A series of papers presented at a conference sponsored by the College Board, the American Association of Collegiate Registrars and Admissions Officers, and the National Association of College Admissions Counselors. A full range of views about marketing and student recruitment is presented. Available from the College Board.

Cope, Robert G. *Strategic Planning, Management, and Decision-Making.* AAHE/ERIC Higher Education Research Report No. 9. Washington, DC: American Association for Higher Education, 1981.

An analytic discussion of strategic planning as it can be applied to higher education. Cope reviews the history of the field and the development of the literature and identifies various applications of strategic planning theory to higher education.

Crossland, Fred E. "Learning to Cope with a Downward Slope" and Frances, Carol, "Apocalyptic vs. Strategic Planning." *Change,* Vol. 12, July-August 1980.

This issue of *Change* presents two different perspectives of institutional futures in the 1980s. Crossland, arguing that demography is destiny, urges faculty and administrators to assess realistically the consequences of enrollment decline in the 1980s and to begin to plan accordingly. Frances, however, suggests that the academic community's "greatest problem (in the 1980s) may not be that we will not be unprepared for the (enrollment) decline, but that we will be so well prepared that we will make it happen." Frances identifies a number of strategies she believes could help to at least maintain and perhaps increase enrollments.

Frances, Carol. *College Enrollment Trends: Testing the Conventional Wisdom Against the Facts.* Washington, DC: American Council on Education, 1980.

Frances presents a concise review of demographic and enrollment trends for the postwar era. She contrasts the consensual wisdom against actual enrollment data for various sectors of higher education. The last portion of her report suggests an optimistic future for higher education in which enrollments experience only marginal decline or even slight growth.

Grabowski, Stanley M. *Marketing in Higher Education.* AAHE/ERIC Higher Education Research Report No. 5. Washington, DC: American Association for Higher Education, 1981.

Grabowski's analytic review of the application of marketing concepts to postsecondary institutions focuses on the components of a marketing plan. He reviews and summarizes such concepts as market segmentation and positioning, product image, market research, pricing policies, etc. He also identifies marketing strategies that have demonstrated their effectiveness in higher education. All of the relevant marketing literature is cited in this monograph.

Ihlanfeldt, William. *Achieving Optimal Enrollments and Tuition Revenues.* San Francisco: Jossey-Bass, 1980.

William Ihlanfeldt, Vice President for Institutional Relations and Dean of Admissions at Northwestern University, has written a handbook for administrators who want to use marketing concepts to enhance recruitment and enrollment planning activities. He reviews such issues as the factors affecting student application and matriculation decisions, and components of an institutional marketing plan. Finally, his volume provides examples of resource and planning materials, such as fee structure and revenue tables, student survey instruments, letters to parents of prospective students, etc.

Leslie, David W., Samuel E. Kellams, and G. Manny Gunne. *Part-Time Faculty in American Higher Education.* New York: Prager, 1982.

Part-time faculty have become a major segment of the academic labor force. Yet few institutions consciously assess the institutional and programmatic consequences of expanding the ranks of part-time faculty. This volume provides a comprehensive assessment of the role of part-time faculty in higher education. Based on the authors' survey and case study research, the volume assesses the educational and policy implications of the growth of part-time faculty during the 1970s.

Mingle, James R. and Associates. *Challenges of Retrenchment.* San Francisco: Jossey-Bass, 1981.

A collection of essays describing and assessing the problems and challenges of retrenchment, emphasizing state policy issues. The work is based in part on extensive case studies sponsored by the Southern Regional Education Board. The issues addressed in this volume include program review and discontinuance. institutional mergers, state budgeting during retrenchment, procedures for faculty retrenchment, and state policy toward private institutions.

Mortimer, Kenneth P. and Michael L. Tierney. *The Three "R's" of the Eighties: Reduction, Reallocation, and Retrenchment.* AAHE/ERIC Higher Education Research Report No. 4. Washington, DC: American Association for Higher Education, 1979.

This monograph reviews the literature on enrollments and finances in the 1970s and 1980s; it also presents case data from their case studies during the late 1970s. Mortimer and Tierney offer recommendations for institutional planning and include a number of checklists, guidelines, and policy documents that can serve as models.

Stadtman, Verne A. *Academic Adaptations,* San Francisco: Jossey-Bass, 1980.

Drawing on case studies and surveys conducted by the Carnegie Council and the Carnegie Commission during the 1970s, Stadtman examines the changes in students, faculty, administrators, and institutional diversity that occurred during the 1970s and identifies some of the strategies institutions have developed to adjust to the demographic challenges of the 1980s.

Bibliography

A Futures Creating Paradigm: A Guide to Long-Range Planning from the Future for the Future. Washington, DC: American Association of State Colleges and Universities, 1978.

Allison, Graham. *The Essence of Decision.* Boston: Little, Brown and Company, 1971.

Astin, Alexander W. *Four Critical Years.* San Francisco: Jossey-Bass, 1977.

Astin, Alexander W. *Preventing Students From Dropping Out.* San Francisco: Jossey-Bass, 1975.

Astin, Alexander W. *Predicting Academic Performance in College.* New York: The Free Press, 1971.

Astin, Alexander W., Margo R. King, and Gerald T. Richardson. *The American College Freshman: National Norms.* Los Angeles: Graduate School of Education, University of California, 1982.

Baldridge, J. Victor. *Power and Conflict in the University.* New York: Wiley, 1971.

Baldridge, J. Victor and Frank R. Kemerer. *Assessing the Impact of Faculty Collective Bargaining.* AAHE-ERIC Higher Education Research Report No. 8. Washington, DC: American Association for Higher Education, 1981.

Baldridge, J. Victor and Michael Tierney. *New Approaches to Management: Creating Practical Systems of Management Information and Management by Objectives.* San Francisco: Jossey-Bass, 1979.

Baldridge, J. Victor, David Curtis, George Ecker, and Gary Riley. *Policy-Making and Effective Leadership.* San Francisco: Jossey-Bass, 1978.

Baldridge, J. Victor, Frank R. Kemerer, and Kenneth C. Green. *Enrollments in the Eighties: Crisis, Myths, and Realities.* AAHE-ERIC/Higher Education Research Report. Washington, DC: American Association of Higher Education, 1982.

Beal, Philip and Lee Noel. *What Works in Student Retention.* Boulder, Colorado: National Center for Higher Education Management Systems, 1980.

Blackburn, James C. "Marketing Admissions: A Perspective on Its Use." *College Board Review,* No. 116, Summer 1980.

Bowen, Howard R. *The Costs of Higher Education*. San Francisco: Jossey-Bass, 1980.

Bowen, Howard R. "Higher Education: A Growth Industry?" *Educational Record*, Vol. 55, Summer 1974: 147-158.

Campbell, Roger. "Avoiding the Prospect of Becoming a Future-Former College President." Speech delivered to the Presidents of Presbyterian Colleges Conference, Washington, DC, February 7, 1981.

Campbell, Roger. "Future Enrollment Goals Via Traditional Institutional Strengths." Speech delivered at the Annual Conference of the American Association of Collegiate Registrars and Admissions Officers, April 22, 1980.

Caren, William A. and Frank R. Kemerer. "The Internal Dimensions of Institutional Marketing." *College and University*, Spring 1979: 173-188.

Carnegie Council on Policy Studies in Higher Education. *Fair Practices in Higher Education*. San Francisco: Jossey-Bass, 1979.

Carnegie Council on Policy Studies in Higher Education. *Three Thousand Futures*. San Francisco: Jossey-Bass, 1980.

Carnegie Foundation for the Advancement of Teaching. *More than Survival: Prospects for Higher Education in a Period of Uncertainty*. San Francisco: Jossey-Bass, 1975.

Centra, John A. "College Enrollment in the 1980s: Projections and Possibilities." *Journal of Higher Education*. Vol. 51, 1980: 18-39.

Chapman, David W. "A Model of Student College Choice," *Journal of Higher Education*, Vol. 52, No. 5, 1981: 490-505.

Chapman, David W. and Russell H. Johnson. *Salaries and Compensation of Admissions Officers*. Skokie, Illinois: National Association of College Admissions Counselors, 1981.

Chapman, David W. and Sandra L. Urbach. "Career Paths of College Admissions Directors." School of Education, State University of New York at Albany, 1982.

Cheit, Carl F. *The New Depression in Higher Education*. New York: McGraw-Hill, 1971.

Cohen, Michael D. and James G. March. *Leadership in Ambiguity*. Berkeley, California: Carnegie Commission on Higher Education, 1974.

The College Board. *National Report on College Bound Seniors, 1981*. New York: College Entrance Examination Board, 1981.

Cope, Robert A. *Strategic Planning, Management, and Decision-Making*. AAHE/ERIC Higher Education Research Report No. 9. Washington, DC: American Association for Higher Education, 1981.

Cosand, Joseph P., "Developing an Institutional Master Plan." In *Improving Academic Management*, Paul Jedamus, Marvin W. Peterson, and associates (eds.), San Francisco: Jossey-Bass, 1980: 164-176.

Dresch, Stephen P. "Demography, Technology, and Higher Education: Toward a Formal Mode of Educational Adaptation." *Journal of Political Economy*, Vol. 83, 1975.

Fenske, Robert, "Setting Institutional Goals and Objectives." In *Improving Academic Management*, Paul Jedamus, Marvin W. Peterson, and associates (eds.), San Francisco: Jossey-Bass, 1980: 177-199.

Fincher, Cameron. "The Packaging of Planning." *Research in Higher Education*, Vol. 11, No. 4, 1979: 365-368.

Finn, Chester E., Jr. "Giving a Boost to Quality Education." *Wall Street Journal*, June 1981a.

Finn, Chester E., Jr. "Toward a New Consensus." *Change*, 13, September, 1981b: 16-20, 60-63.

Finn, Chester E., Jr. "Dollars, Scholars, and Bureaucrats." Washington, DC: Brookings Institution, 1978.

Fram, Eugene. "Organizing the Marketing Focus in Higher Education." Paper presented at the Annual Forum of the Association of Institutional Research, May 1975.

Freeman, Richard B. *Youth Employment Opportunities: Changes in Relative Position of College and High School Graduates*. Presentation at Temple University Conference on "Improving Labor Market Information," October 21, 1974.

Friedlander, Jack. "Institutional Practices of Part-Time Faculty" In *Using Part-Time Faculty Effectively*, Michael H. Parsons (ed.). San Francisco: Jossey-Bass, 1980.

Froomkin, Joseph. *Changing Credential Objectives of Students in Post-Secondary Education*. Washington, DC: U.S. Dept. of Health, Education, and Welfare, Contract No. 0574257, 1974.

Furman, James R. "State Budgeting and Retrenchment." In *Challenges of Retrenchment*. James R. Mingle and associates. San Francisco: Jossey-Bass, 1981.

Glenny, Lyman A. "Demographic and Related Issues for Higher Education in the 1980s." *Journal of Higher Education*, Vol. 51, 1980: 363-380.

Glenny, Lyman A. and Frank M. Bowen. "Warning Signals of Distress." In *Challenges of Retrenchment*, James R. Mingle and associates. San Francisco: Jossey-Bass, 1981: 32-47.

Glenny, Lyman A., John R. Shea, Janet H. Ruyle, and Kathryn H. Freschi. *Presidents Confront Reality*, San Francisco: Jossey-Bass, 1976.

Grabowski, Stanley M. *Marketing in Higher Education*. AAHE/ERIC Higher Education Research Report No. 5. Washington, DC: American Association for Higher Education, 1981.

Grant, Gerald and David Riesman. *The Perpetual Dream*. Chicago: University of Chicago Press, 1978.

Green, Kenneth C. "Program Review and the State Responsibility for Higher Education." *Journal of Higher Education,* Vol. 52, 1981: 67-80.

Hartnett, Rodney and Robert A. Feldmesser. "College Admissions Testing and the Myth of Selectivity: Unresolved Questions and Needed Research." American Association for Higher Education *Bulletin,* 1980.

Henson, James W. *Test Score Decline and the Distribution of Institutional Quality.* Los Angeles: Higher Education Research Institute, University of California, forthcoming.

Hobbs, John M. and Donald F. Heany. "Coupling Strategy to Operating Plans," *Harvard Business Review,* May-June, 1977: 119-126.

Huddleston, Thomas, Jr. and Burt F. Batty. "Marketing Financial Aid." In *Marketing Higher Education,* David W. Barton, Jr. (ed.). New Directions for Higher Education, No. 21. San Francisco: Jossey-Bass, 1978: 37-50.

Ihlanfeldt, William. *Achieving Optimal Enrollments and Tuition Revenues.* San Francisco: Jossey-Bass, 1980.

Katz, Daniel and Robert Kahn. *The Social Psychology of Organizations.* New York: Wiley and Sons, 1966.

Kemerer, Frank R. and J. Victor Baldridge. *Unions on Campus.* San Francisco: Jossey-Bass, 1976.

Kotler, Phillip. "Applying Marketing Theory to College Admissions." In *A Role for Marketing in College Admissions.* New York: College Entrance Examination Board, 1976.

Johnson, R. H. and David W. Chapman. "College Recruitment Literature: Does the Student Understand it?" *Research in Higher Education.* Vol. 11. 1979: 309-319.

Kotler, Philip. *Marketing for Non-Profit Organizations.* Englewood Cliffs, New Jersey: Prentice-Hall, 1975.

Kotler, Philip and Patrick E. Murphy. "Strategic Planning for Higher Education." *Journal of Higher Education,* Vol. 52, No. 5, 1981: 470-489.

Kreutner, Leonard and Eric S. Godfrey. "Enrollment Management: A New Vehicle for Institutional Renewal." *College Board Review,* No. 118, Winter 1980-81: 6-9, 29.

Lawrence, Judith K. and Kenneth C. Green. *A Question of Quality: The Higher Education Ratings Game.* AAHE-ERIC/Higher Educational Research Report No. 5. Washington, DC: American Association for Higher Education, 1980.

Lenning, Oscar T., Phillip E. Beal, and Ken Saver. *Retention and Attrition: Evidence for Research and Action.* Boulder, Colorado: National Center for Higher Education Management Systems, 1980.

Leslie, David W., Samuel E. Kellams, and G. Manny Gunne. *Part-Time Faculty in American Higher Education.* New York: Prager, 1982.

Leslie, Larry L., and Howard F. Miller, Jr. *Higher Education and the Steady State*. AAHE/ERIC Higher Education Research Report No. 4. Washington: American Association for Higher Education, 1974.

Levine, Arthur. *Why Innovation Fails*. Albany, New York: State University of New York Press, 1981.

Litton, Harry H. "Messages and Media; Toward Enhanced Performance in Communicating with Parents and Prospective Students." ERIC Clearinghouse for Higher Education, 1981. ED-208-708.

Minter, John and Howard Bowen. "Assessing Their Institutions. College Presidents Express 'Extraordinarily High' Levels of Confidence." *Chronicle of Higher Education*, 1981. ED-208-708.

Mortimer, Kenneth P. *Accountability*. AAHE-ERIC/Higher Education Research Report No. 1. Washington, DC: American Association for Higher Education, 1972.

Murphy, Patrick E. and Richard J. McGarrity. "Marketing Universities: A Survey of Student Recruitment Activities." *College and University*. Vol. 53, Spring 1978: 249-261.

National Center for Education Statistics. *The Condition of Education, 1981*. Washington, DC: U.S. Government Printing Office, 1981.

National Center for Education Statistics. *Projections of Education: Statistics to 1986-87*. Washington, DC: U.S. Government Printing Office, 1976.

O'Toole, James. *Working, Learning, and the American Future*. San Francisco: Jossey-Bass, 1977.

O'Toole, James, William W. Van Alstyne, and Richard Chait. *Three Views: Tenure*. New Rochelle, New York: *Change* Magazine Press, 1980.

Peterson, Marvin W. "Analyzing Alternative Approaches to Planning." In *Improving Academic Management*, Paul Jedamus, Marvin W. Peterson, and associates (eds.). San Francisco: Jossey-Bass Publishers, 1980: 113-163.

Riesman, David. *On Higher Education*. San Francisco: Jossey-Bass, 1980.

Riesman, David. "New College." *Change*, Vol. 7, May 1975, 34-43.

Shulman, Carol Herrnstadt. *Enrollment Trends in Higher Education*. AAHE/ERIC Higher Education Research Report No. 6. Washington: American Association for Higher Education, 1976.

Silvers, Philip A. "The Role and Operation of Visiting Accreditation Teams." American Association of Higher Education *Bulletin*, May 1982: 13-16.

Solmon, Lewis C., Laura Kent, Nancy L. Ochsner, and Margo-Lea Hurwicz. *Underemployed PhDs*. Lexington, Massachusetts: Lexington Books, 1981.

Spence, David S. and George B. Weathersby. "Changing Patterns of State Funding." In *Challenges of Retrenchment*, James R. Mingle and Associates. San Francisco: Jossey-Bass, 1981: 226-243.

Stadtman, Verne A. *Academic Adaptations: Higher Education Prepares for the 1980s and 1990s.* A Report for the Carnegie Council on Policy Studies in Higher Education. San Francisco: Jossey-Bass, 1980.

Stauffer, Thomas M. "The Neoconservative Challenge to Higher Education." *Educational Record,* Vol. 62, Spring, 1981.

Tierney, Michael. "An Estimate of Departmental Cost Functions." *Higher Education,* Vol. 9, 1980: 453-468.

Troutt, William E. "Regional Accreditation Evaluative Criteria and Quality Assurance." *Journal of Higher Education,* Vol. 50, 1979: 199-210.

Undergraduate Admissions: The Realities of Institutional Policies, Practices, and Procedures. New York: College Entrance Examination Board, 1980.

Urbach, Sandra L. and David W. Chapman. "Other Grass is Greener: The Career Paths of Admissions Staff." Albany, New York: State University of New York at Albany, 1982.

Veysey, Lawrence. "Undergraduate Admissions: Past and Future." In *Marketing in College Admissions: A Broadening of Perspectives.* New York: College Entrance Examination Board, 1980.

Western Interstate Commission for Higher Education. *Getting Into College: A Survey of Changing Admission Requirements in Western Public Higher Education.* Boulder, Colorado: The Commission, 1982.

Western Interstate Commission on Higher Education. *High School Graduates: Projections for the Fifty States.* Boulder, Colorado: The Commission, 1979.